THE
MULTICULTURAL
WORKSHOP

BOOK 1

Linda Lonon Blanton
Linda Lee

Heinle & Heinle Publishers
A Division of Wadsworth Inc.
Boston, Massachusetts 02116 U.S.A.

The publication of *The Multicultural Workshop, Book 1* was directed by the members of the Newbury House Publishing Team at Heinle & Heinle:

Erik Gundersen, Editorial Director
Kristin Thalheimer, Production Editor

Also participating in the publication of this program were:

Publisher: Stanley J. Galek
Editorial Production Manager: Elizabeth Holthaus
Project Manager: Angela Malovich Castro, English Language Trainers
Assistant Editor: Karen P. Hazar
Associate Marketing Manager: Donna Hamilton
Production Assistant: Maryellen Eschmann
Manufacturing Coordinator: Mary Beth Lynch
Interior Designer and Compositor: Greta D. Sibley
Illustrators: Anne O'Brien, Stephanie Peterson, Len Shalansky
Cover Artist: James Steinberg
Cover Designer: Bortman Design Group
Photo Coordinator: Martha Liebs-Heckly
Photo Researcher: Carl Spector

Library of Congress Cataloging-in-Publication Data
Blanton, Linda Lonon, 1942–
      The multicultural workshop : a reading and writing program. Book
   1 / Linda Lonon Blanton, Linda Lee.
           p.   cm.
       ISBN 0-8384-4834-8
       1. English language--Textbooks for foreign speakers.   I. Lee,
   Linda.   II. Title.
   PE1128.B59215   1994
   428.2'4--dc20   93-39447
                                                                          CIP

Heinle & Heinle Publishers is a division of Wadsworth, Inc.

Manufactured in the United States of America

ISBN 0-8384-4834-8

10   9   8   7   6   5   4   3   2

A Special Thanks

The authors and publisher would like to thank the following individuals who reviewed and/or field-tested *The Multicultural Workshop* at various stages of its development and who offered many helpful insights and suggestions:

Judith L. Paiva, *Northern Virginia Community College*
Cheryl Benz, *Miami-Dade Community College*
Brad Stocker, *Miami-Dade Community College*
Lorin Leith, *Santa Rosa Junior College (CA)*
Joe McVeigh, *California State University, Los Angeles*
Heather Robertson, *California State University, Los Angeles*
Tom Coles, *Arizona State University*
Adrianne Saltz, *Boston University*
Jamie Beaton, *Boston University*
John Dennis, *San Francisco State University, Emeritus*
Virginia Herringer, *Pasadena City College*
Virginia Gibbons, *Oakton Community College (IL)*
Danielle Dibie, *California State University, Northridge*
Helen Harper, *American Language Institute, New York University*
Bernadette Garcia Budd, *Suffolk County Community College (NJ)*
Julietta Ruppert, *Houston Community College*
Elizabeth Templin, *University of Arizona*
Charles Schroen, *The Pennsylvania State University*
Betty Speyrer, *Delgado Community College (LA)*
Marjorie Vai, *The New School for Social Research*
Marianne Phinney, *University of Texas, El Paso*
Eve Chambers Sanchez, *Oregon State University*
Vivian Wind Aronow, *College of Staten Island (City University of New York)*
Luke Bailey, *University of Hawaii at Hilo*
Martha Low, *University of Oregon*
Virginia Vogel Zanger, *Boston University*
Lois Spitzer, *Atlantic Community College (NJ)*
Fredericka Stoller, *Northern Arizona University*
Wendy Hyman-Fite, *Washington University in St. Louis*
Peggy Anderson, *Wichita State University*
Pat Holdcraft, *University of Miami*
Kim Smith, *University of Texas, Austin*
Sally LaLuzerne-Oi, *Hawaii Pacific University*
Elizabeth Byleen, *University of Kansas*
Mac Toll, *Colorado School of Mines & University of Colorado at Boulder*

CONTENTS

Unit One: Identity 2

GUIDE TO STRATEGIES

The Multicultural Workshop *Program*

The Multicultural Workshop is a fully integrated reading and writing program for adult students of English as a second language. The program is based on an interactive pedagogy that values collaboration and meaningful communication as powerful tools for learning. In practice, the pedagogy takes the form of classroom activities in which students discuss, read, and write together—always within a thematic context that provides topical substance, intellectual interest, and linguistic coherence.

The Multicultural Workshop: Book 1 is designed for high-beginning ESL students. *Book 1* is followed by *Books 2* and *3,* written for low-to-mid intermediate and mid-to-high intermediate ESL students, respectively. In *Book 1,* students begin to build a foundation for the critical literacy needed for academic study. In *Books 2* and *3,* they continue building on what they have learned in *Book 1* as they become more and more involved in the kinds of reading and writing work required of them in the academic mainstream.

While the same five themes—**identity, change, choices, relationships,** and **conflict**—integrate the series, the focus within a given thematic area shifts from book to book. For example, in *Book 1,* students focus on **change** as an individual phenomenon; in *Book 2,* **change** is analyzed as an environmental process; in *Book 3,* the theme of **change** is viewed through a social and political perspective. This format allows for integration and a growing sophistication in students' work.

A resource box containing over a hundred complementary readings is an integral part of the *Multicultural Workshop* program. Designed to bring the library into the classroom, the box holds a wide range of readings on cards, charts for recording students' progress through the box, and answer keys to the questions following the readings. Graded by level of difficulty, the readings range from a level easily accessible to students using *Book 1* to a level fairly challenging for students using *Book 3.* In other words, no matter which textbook of the

Multicultural Workshop series students are working through, they will find plenty of additional readings in the resource box.

A teacher's resource guide, housed in the resource box and designed to accompany the textbooks, contains black-line masters for supplementing students' class work in various aspects of grammar and writing mechanics. We have included these resources for teachers to use when students need directed work in an aspect of language usage that they seem not to be "picking up." The teacher's guide also contains teaching tips, mini-lessons, suggestions for additional classroom activities, and explanations that might be of value to new teachers or to experienced teachers who are new to a workshop approach.

We are grateful to Erik Gundersen, ESL Editor for college/intensive programs at Heinle & Heinle, for his help and encouragement on this project. It was during a brainstorming session with Erik at a TESOL Conference that we first got the idea for the *Multicultural Workshop* program; he has remained steadfast in his support throughout its evolution. We also want to thank Betty Speyrer, a teacher at Delgado Community College in New Orleans, whose students taught us a lot about *The Multicultural Workshop*.

The Multicultural Workshop: Book 1 is a reading and writing program for high-beginning adult students of English as a second language. Like the whole *Multicultural Workshop* series, *Book 1* is based on an interactive pedagogy that values collaboration and meaningful communication as powerful tools for learning. In practice, the pedagogy takes the form of classroom activities in which students discuss, read, and write together—always within a thematic context.

In the pages that follow, we offer discussions of the philosophical underpinnings of *The Multicultural Workshop,* as well as plenty of practical information designed to make teaching with this program satisfying, effective, and enjoyable.

Overview of The Multicultural Workshop: Book 1

❖ **GOALS.** *The Multicultural Workshop: Book 1* is designed to do the following:

- increase students' overall fluency in English

- raise students' reading and writing proficiencies

- increase students' vocabulary

- help students develop strategies for critical thinking

- help students develop strategies for reading and writing as college students are expected to do

- establish the foundation for academic literacy, required for students' success in college study

Field testing showed us, additionally, that ESL students using *The Multicultural Workshop: Book 1* acquire an eagerness to participate in their own learning; an awareness of their individual responsiblity as readers and writers in the communication process; and an understanding of the essential role of their own insights, opinions, knowledge, and experience in responding to others' texts and in producing their own.

In observing students using *The Multicultural Workshop: Book 1,* we were pleased to see how much fun they were having, how eager they were to read and write, and how quickly their command of English grew. They became more critical and focused in their thinking, more insightful and analytic about life around them, and more connected to and invested in the texts they were reading.

❖ **UNITS AND THEMES.** *The Multicultural Workshop: Book 1* comprises five units, each designed around a different theme. The themes—**identity, change, choices, relationships,** and **conflict**—are universal and timeless, allowing students to ask meaningful questions and explore issues that concern all of us as human beings. However, since we are all shaped by our particular cultures and life experiences, answers to the questions we ask and our articulation of the issues that concern us differ from person to person.

The Multicultural Workshop: Book 1 directs students to approach these differences analytically and respectfully, building on the rich cultural environment of the classroom to promote and develop critical thinking skills and the strategies needed by students to explore their differences (and similarities) through reading and writing. Field testing showed us that the themes work well in providing a context for limited-English students to draw from their varied backgrounds—to discuss and read and write about what they know—without intrusion into their personal lives.

❖ **CHAPTERS AND THEMES.** Each unit of *The Multicultural Workshop: Book 1* comprises four chapters, designed around a different aspect of the unit theme. For example, Chapter 1 in Unit 1—the unit on identity—explores the question "Who are you?," while Chapters 2, 3, and 4 ask "What do we have in common?," What do actions reveal?," and "What makes up a life story?" Readings in each chapter—poems, folk tales, newspaper articles, student writings, and expository pieces—connect to the theme and invite its exploration.

❖ **FINAL PROJECT OF EACH UNIT.** Each unit ends with a summative writing activity, called the "final project." Here, students select a draft from their writing folders for further work from among pieces of writing drafted during the course of the unit. Supported by writing samples from other ESL writers, reflections on the writing process by an L1 writer, and tips for writers, students are guided to revise pieces they have written in that particular unit.

❖ **ACTIVITIES.** The activities built into each unit are varied: some require solo work; some, small group work or pair work; some involve the whole class; others direct students to make entries in their journals; still others request that students complete a draft for their writing folders. Across activities, students are listening, speaking, reading, and writing. Some activities requiring writing can be completed in the textbook—and space is provided; some can be best completed on the board; others require students to use their own notebook paper. In addition to the textbook, then, each student needs a separate notebook to serve as a journal, a manila folder or an accordion file to serve as a writing folder, and a supply of notebook paper.

❖ **REFERENCE GUIDE.** At the back of *The Multicultural Workshop: Book 1* is a reference guide, keyed to the reading, writing, and critical thinking strategies highlighted in small boxes throughout the units. The guide explains each strategy, gives examples and illustrations, and defines terms. Overall, the reference guide provides significant information that student writers need to know—not only to complete the tasks in *The Multicultural Workshop: Book 1* but to understand what proficient readers and writers do.

For example, the first task in Chapter 2 of Unit 2 requires brainstorming. The small box to the right of the activity instructs students wanting to know more about brainstorming to turn to page 169 of the Reference Guide. On that page, students can inform themselves of what brainstorming is, how it works, and what purpose it serves; they can also see an example of the kinds of ideas brainstorming can produce. The reference guide serves as a handy tool, and it allows the work in the body of the textbook to remain uncluttered and free of the instructional apparatus that often gets in students' way.

How Does The Multicultural Workshop *Play Out in the Classroom?*

❖ **WORKSHOP APPROACH.** A workshop classroom requires students to move around for small group work and pairwork. At times, students are all talking at once—in their respective groups. Some activities direct students to role-play, dramatize, or pantomime events and actions. At other times, some students are writing, while others are reading aloud what they have written to classmates serving as listener-readers. Overall, then, more energy is expended, more talking goes on, and more action takes place in a workshop classroom.

In our field testing, we also heard a lot of laughter, saw many smiles, and observed faces intent on listening to what their classmates had to say. We were impressed by students' respect for each other's opinions and by their willingness to listen even when a classmate talked at length. Participating in the field testing were students from Vietnam, Korea, Central and South America, and the Middle East.

The workshop approach is based on the theoretical tenets of collaborative learning and on language acquisition theory, both supporting the notion that students learn in general—and learn to read, speak, and write a language, in particular—through interacting with others in meaningful ways. A learner's intent to communicate must drive each interaction; otherwise, no learning takes place. Meaningful communication requires communicative activities: hence, the workshop classroom, with its collaborative tasks, shared writing, discussions, and reader-response groups.

❖ **ORIENTATION FOR STUDENTS.** The workshop approach may be fairly new to many ESL students. Students may enter ESL classes with the point of view that every scrap of writing must not only be read but corrected by the teacher; that they can only learn from the teacher, the figure of authority; and that their classmates, whose English is not perfect, have nothing to offer them.

We urge you to explain to students that workshop methodology is theoretically sound; that they will get far more practice in groups and pairs than if class time is divided by the total number of students enrolled; that the materials have been successfully tested on students just like them; and that a new approach is always awkward at the beginning. Ultimately, you may need to ask them to give the approach a chance, based on the philosophy of "Try it. You'll like it."

To teachers who have never used a workshop approach in ESL classes, we offer the same philosophy. It takes a while for both teachers and students to "get the hang" of a workshop. We urge you not to abandon certain kinds of activities that seem unsuccessful the first or second time you try them. For example, in the field testing, students had difficulty with inferencing activities at the beginning. However, after the teacher modeled the activity, gave some examples, and "talked" students through the process, they had no more trouble with it. Let students know that it is normal to have difficulty with something that is new—and then carry on.

❖ **GROUP WORK.** We offer the following tips on group work:

• Groups of 3–4 seem to work best.

• Mix languages; this establishes English as a valid "lingua franca."

• Mix strengths and weaknesses.

• To get the mixes indicated above, you may need to be the one dividing up the class. However, if the mixes are not a problem, students can choose their own groups.

• With group work requiring continuity, keep the same groupings; change groupings when students start a new cycle of work.

• Insist on "good neighbor" rules within groups: respect everyone's contribution; encourage everyone to participate; give feedback to each other.

• The teacher circulates during group work. When you hear or see something praiseworthy, point it out. Students learn the dynamics of positive group work in this way.

Reading in **The Multicultural Workshop: Book 1**

❖ **VARIED GENRES.** The readings in each unit relate to the unit theme and, in particular, to the aspect of the theme focused on in a particular chapter. The readings, all selected for their potential interest to culturally diverse groups of students, are representative of many genres: poems, folk tales, newspaper articles, biographies, and expository pieces. ESL students at the high-beginning level need to build a broad base of reading fluency and literacy across a myriad of readings before they focus on the kinds of academic readings they will be required to manage—in volume—in their mainstream courses. *The Multicultural Workshop: Books 2* and *3* ease students into the academic genre, while *The Multicultural Workshop: Book 1* helps them develop the strategies necessary to handle it.

❖ **READING COMPREHENSION.** The readings in *The Multicultural Workshop: Book 1* provide contexts within which students interact; the readings do not serve as models for student writing, although we fully expect students to internalize aspects of the language of the readings as they work their way through the textbook. Following a reading, various activities prompt students to tie in their own knowledge, experiences, and opinions—as all proficient readers do—in order to build a framework for comprehension of the reading. Students are also called on to bring the connections they are building into their writing, as they begin to analyze their own views and experiences against others' perceptions of related experiences.

❖ **READING STRATEGIES.** In our experience, some students comprehend little when they read because, in part, they have developed few strategies for creating comprehension for themselves. A great deal of the focus in *The Multicultural Workshop: Book 1* is on helping students develop these strategies, among which are the following:

- predicting
- paraphrasing
- scanning
- interpreting
- inferencing

- summarizing
- finding main ideas
- asking questions
- taking notes
- previewing

A complete listing of all strategies built into the activities of *The Multicultural Workshop: Book 1* can be found in a guide on page ix of the book.

❖ **APPROACH TO READINGS.** At first glance, the readings in each unit appear more difficult than one might expect high-beginning ESL students to be able to handle. Our field testing shows that these readings are not out of students' reach. In reviewing the readings in *The Multicultural Workshop: Book 1*, it is important for you to keep in mind that we are asking students to **respond** to the readings; the readings are not there to be "learned." That students cannot write the texts we are asking them to read does not mean that they cannot work with mature and sophisticated concepts and information embodied in the readings. Our experience with the methodology and with these readings tells us that this is so.

❖ **USING THE RESOURCE BOX.** The readings in the resource box provide a number of benefits to students: they provide reading experience additional to the textbook; they motivate students by allowing a choice of readings and a sense of self-directed progress as students chart their way through the box; and the questions that follow the readings reinforce and expand the strategies introduced and used in the textbook activities.

The readings in the resource box can be used by teachers and students in a number of ways. For a class that meets three days a week or more, one class period each week can be designated "free reading day," with students choosing their readings and working independently with the box. For programs that have a separate reading lab, students can be encouraged or required to work with the box outside of class and on their own time.

Writing in **The Multicultural Workshop: Book 1**

❖ **WRITERS' NEEDS.** The writing activities in *The Multicultural Workshop: Book 1* are based on our convictions about the writing needs of high-beginning ESL students preparing to enter the academic mainstream. Some of these needs relate to the kinds of texts students produce; others, to the way they go about producing them. As we see it, student writers at this level of proficiency need the following:

- to gain greater fluency in writing

- to develop their own individual voices

- to connect to their own individual base of knowledge and experiences—to what they know

- to gain an awareness of writing as a process, with revising as a central aspect of that process

- to acquire strategies for creating the process

- to begin "layering" their writing through evaluating, analyzing, summarizing, etc. in order to provide a writer's perspective on the subject matter of the writing; in other words, to begin to do more than simply report

- to have fun and to achieve a measure of success in order to be motivated to continue the hard job of becoming better writers

The writing activities in *The Multicultural Workshop: Book 1* are designed to meet these needs without overwhelming or intimidating high-beginning students. By design, the writing activities do not look like traditional academic tasks, yet they help students develop the sophisticated strategies they will need in their future academic studies.

❖ **WRITING JOURNALS.** Throughout *The Multicultural Workshop: Book 1,* students are directed to make entries in their writing journals. The journal is probably, in actuality, a spiral notebook; in any case, it should be separate from other notebooks in which students take class notes, write their assignments, etc. In their journals, students are encouraged to collect ideas and information for their writing, try out new ideas and new language in writing, and explore ideas they may want to pursue later.

Basically, the journal is a place for writers to store their thoughts and experiment in putting them into words. We strongly urge that journal entries never be corrected or graded. In fact, you may prefer not even to collect students' journals. If you feel, however, that it is important to your students that you read their entries, we urge you to respond as a reader and not critique their writing.

You might read and respond randomly with comments such as "I like this idea!" "What a great plan!" "I know what you mean," where appropriate; you might also respond with references to your own ideas and experience, with comments such as "The same thing happened to me!" or "My childhood was very different from yours. We lived on a farm." In our experience, students seem more invested in keeping a journal if they know they will have a reader. Overall, though, the basic point is this: every writer needs to keep a journal, whether or not it is read by someone else.

❖ **WRITING FOLDERS.** At the end of each chapter in *The Multicultural Workshop: Book 1,* students have a writing assignment that, when completed, they will place in their writing folders. The assignment relates to the work of the chapter, and directions for completing each assignment are given, although students always have latitude as to what they actually write. Latitude is important here: each writer has to be free to come up with what she/he wants to say; otherwise, the writing is sterile and meaningless. If students interpret the directions differently and veer in different directions in completing the assignment, that is no problem.

The writing completed at the end of each chapter becomes a first draft in the writing folder. It should be dated and numbered by the unit and chapter of the textbook—for example, "February 15, 1994, Unit 1, Chapter 2, Draft 1." By the end of each unit, then, writers have completed four first drafts. Whether or not a draft gets more work depends on the writer's interest in that piece of writing.

To complete the final project of each unit, students choose one piece of writing from their writing folders for further work. Urge them to choose one that really interests them, one they are willing to put more effort and energy into. It may not be the draft you would choose, but the choice should be left to the individual writer.

It is while working on their final project for the unit that students learn the lessons all writers must learn: revising is plain hard work. It may take three, four, five (or more) drafts for a writer to work out what he/she wants to say; and with each draft, the writer discovers more about the subject matter of the writing.

❖ **FEEDBACK.** We recommend that, if possible, you meet with students in individual conferences during this drafting period to give them feedback and direction for further revising. Student writers want to know what they are doing well and where they need to improve. Overall, though, we urge you to focus on effort and improvement; perfection from high-beginning ESL writers should not be expected and unreasonably high standards for grammatical accuracy can stifle a developing writer.

It is important to remember that ESL students at this level of proficiency are in the **process of becoming** writers, readers, and speakers of English; they are not there yet. The process is developmental and incremental; and it requires constant internal adjustment and readjustment on the learner's part. And, as ESL teachers know, it requires patience, faith, good will, and a long-range perspective on the teacher's part.

Students' last drafts in each writing cycle should be collected, copied, and placed in a special booklet—a binder or folder—for everyone in the class to read. This sharing of writing provides a crucial benefit to writers, especially developing writers: it establishes a sense of community, a bond, that works in subtle ways to promote better writing.

❖ **SUMMARY: JOURNAL AND WRITING FOLDER.** For easy access, a summary of key points about the journal and writing folder follows:

• Each student needs a special notebook to serve as a writing journal.

• As students work through each chapter of the textbook, they are directed to write in their journals, although they can also be encouraged to make entries on their own.

• Writers use journals to store ideas and information and to experiment with putting them into writing.

• Students' journals should not be corrected or graded; if collected, the teacher should respond as a reader to students' entries.

- Journal entries should be dated.

- Each student needs a manila folder or an accordion file to serve as a writing folder.

- A writing assignment at the end of each chapter goes into the writing folder as a first draft, when completed.

- At the end of each fourth chapter, students choose one of their first drafts for further drafting. This is the "final project" of the unit.

- All drafts in the writing folder should be dated and numbered.

- Individual student conferences are essential during the revising process, while students are completing their end projects.

- Teacher evaluation of students' writing should focus on effort and improvement.

Student Evaluation

❖ **EVALUATING THE WRITING FOLDER.** Students using *The Multicultural Workshop: Book 1* can be best evaluated at the end of the semester on the basis of their writing folders. Here, the evaluator needs to view a student's work across the whole academic term—from first to last entry in the folder—and to also analyze a student's process of revising across the drafts of a multi-draft piece of writing, particularly one completed toward the end of the term.

❖ **EVALUATING WRITING.** While an increasing control over sentence-level grammar is important for high-beginning ESL students, other aspects of their writing are of equal importance. We urge you to keep the following questions in mind when evaluating a student's writing:

- Has the writer begun to develop a distinct voice?

- Does the writer pass beyond simply reporting events to analyzing their importance in the overall context of the writing?

- Does the writer know to establish a limited number of key points?

- Does the writer show an increasing awareness of an audience by explaining, illustrating, giving examples, or in some way amplifying important points?

- Does the writer use clear language?

- Does the writer attempt to make her/his writing interesting? Are details vivid? Are examples relevant?

- Can a reader follow the writer's thinking and arrangement of ideas?

- Has the writer begun to develop a clear sense of an introduction, body, and conclusion, where appropriate?

- Does the writer show a sense of being able to make positive changes in any of the aspects above, over the course of several drafts? In other words, is the writer beginning to revise his/her writing?

High-beginning students will not be perfect writers by the end of the term using any materials, but improvements in the areas indicated above are to be applauded and rewarded—and students will want to know where they are improving.

❖ **EVALUATING READING.** If the classroom teacher is expected to evaluate students' reading proficiency, we suggest the following: select two or three reading cards for each student from the resource box, choosing from the front end of the box for high-beginning students. Of those 3–4 chosen at random by the teacher, ask the student to choose whichever one she/he likes best, read it, and write to a classmate, telling enough about the reading to interest the classmate and explaining why the reader thinks the classmate should want to read it. Then collect each student's writing, keeping a student's "review" together with the particular reading. As you read a student's writing, we suggest you keep these questions in mind:

- Does the reader show that she/he is able to follow the reading?

- Does the reader synthesize enough of the reading to be able to tell someone else about it?

- Does the reader show evidence of discerning certain aspects of the reading that might interest another reader?

- Does the reader bring his/her own views to bear on the reading? Does the reader use those views to make sense of the reading? Does the reader relate any aspect of this particular reading to other readings?

If you discern some of these complexities in students' responses to readings, then your students are on their way to becoming proficient readers.

❖ **OTHER EVALUATION SCENARIOS.** End-of-term evaluation proce-
dures vary greatly from program to program, so the scenario detailed
above—with the classroom teacher evaluating students' writing and/or
reading—may not apply. While we think it ideal for students using *The
Multicultural Workshop: Book 1* to be evaluated on the basis of their
classwork, other scenarios are possible:

- In programs with portfolio assessment, the scenario is barely different
  from the one above for evaluating writing. Students' writing folders
  are their portfolios, and someone other than the classroom teacher
  usually serves as evaluator.

- In programs with a proficiency examination serving to determine
  course grades and future placement, a student's writing folder might
  be considered by an "appeals" committee in cases where the classroom teacher knows that the exam results do not give a true reading
  of a student's proficiencies.

- In some programs, proficiency examination results might be com-
  bined with a student's course work—for workshop students, the writing and/or reading evaluation detailed above—to determine the
  course grade and future placement.

- In programs with competency-based assessment, the index of reading, writing, and critical thinking strategies at the back of the
  Multicultural Workshop: Book 1 can help determine the match
  between the skills required by a program curriculum and those
  employed by workshop students. In this scenario, an examination
  might need to be constructed by teachers, using the workshop materials to test to what degree of proficiency students use the strategies.

Authors' Invitation

Teachers across the United States have provided input to the cre-
ation of *The Multicultural Workshop* program—through the review
process and field testing of the materials. Perhaps because we, ourselves, are ESL teachers, we feel that ESL teachers know best what
works in the classroom; and we have benefited greatly from other
teachers' suggestions. If you have questions about the materials or,
after using them, have feedback that you would be willing to give us,
we would be happy to hear from you. Please write to us at the following address: Linda Lonon Blanton and Linda Lee, Heinle & Heinle
Publishers, 20 Park Plaza, Boston, MA 02116.

The Multicultural Workshop provides a collection of readings (folk tales, poems, newspaper articles, excerpts from books, and student writing) as well as writing and discussion activities. Each of the readings and activities relates to one of five themes:

- Identity

- Change

- Choices

- Relationships

- Conflict

UNIT THREE
Choices

In this unit you will read four selections related to the theme of choice.

- What are some of the choices people make at different times in their lives?
- Which are the hardest choices? Why?

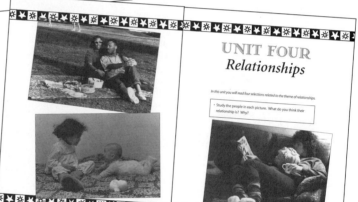

UNIT FOUR
Relationships

In this unit you will read four selections related to the theme of relationships.

- Study the people in each picture. What do you think their relationship is? Why?

Francisco Goya, 3 May 1808

UNIT FIVE
Conflict

In this unit you will read four selections related to the theme of conflict.

- What does the word conflict mean to you?

What You Will Be Doing in **The Multicultural Workshop**

Throughout this program you will be reading, writing, and discussing ideas with your classmates.

Sometimes you will write your ideas in your journal.

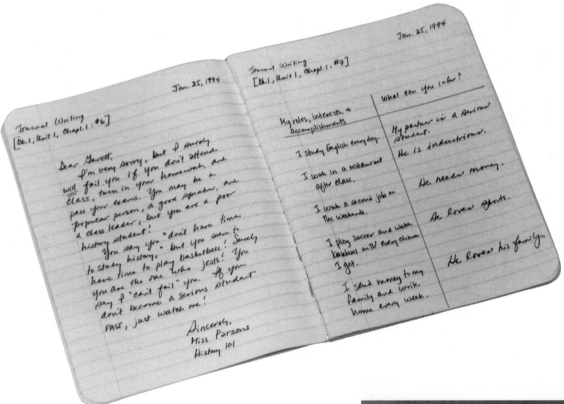

Your journal is your personal notebook. You can list ideas, take notes, draw, or do whatever you want in your journal. Your journal writing will not be corrected.

   Sometimes you will discuss ideas with a partner or with a group of classmates. Sometimes you will do a "Read Around." In a "Read Around" you get together with a group of classmates and take turns reading each other's writing.

In each unit you will also complete four writing assignments. These pieces of writing will go into your writing folder. At the end of each unit, you will select one paper to revise. (You will learn more about the revision process at the end of each unit.) Your teacher will use your revised writing to help you evaluate your progress.

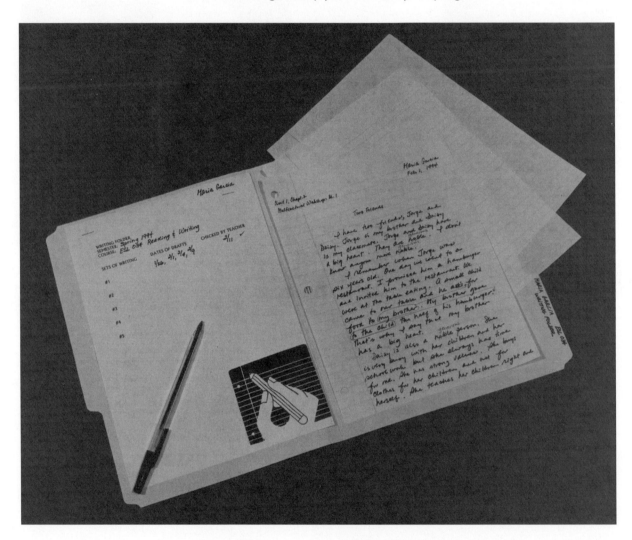

On pages 169–191, you will find a Reference Guide. This section identifies some of the strategies you can use to improve your reading and writing.

Sometimes the hardest part of writing is just getting started. We asked a friend and experienced writer to share her thoughts on getting started:

One Writer's View on Getting Started

The last thing I want to do when I'm having a bad day is to sit down and begin an essay. I have my topic, but what in the world do I want to say about it? Why, why, why did the teacher assign us *this* topic. Ugh. I grumble and groan. I walk around my apartment and water plants. I stand on the front porch and watch the neighbor mow her lawn. I'm simply putting off what I know I'll have to do later.

But walking around isn't always the worst thing, I've decided. Sometimes I'll shut my bedroom door, pace back and forth, and talk to myself. I call this "brainstorming out loud."

Sometimes I begin by "word doodling." I look over the assignment and start filling up a piece of paper with key words from the teacher's assignment. Then I add my own words, all that I can think of, that connect to the assignment. I write down memories, rhyming words, antonyms of the key words. Occasionally I'll find that I have a place to start when the paper is full. Other times I realize that some junk in my head needed to get out before I could get down to work.

Other times I start with my readings. If I'm writing about other articles or essays, I'll take them all out. The floor or a big table is a good place to do this. I fill a blank sheet of paper with all the important sentences or words that I underlined or highlighted in these texts. Then I start over again with another piece of paper and try to group these important words and issues together in columns or squares on the page. Almost always some things start to seem more interesting or more related to the assignment.

Sometimes I simply look up the definition of a word in the dictionary. This may give me direction. A friend of mine insists that her best writing inspiration comes when she walks her dog in the evening. Other writers I know carry a notebook with them when they take a bath, talk on the phone, or go shopping.

■❋✦❋✦❋✦❋✦❋■

ABOUT THE AUTHOR
Amanda Buege is a graduate student at the University of New Orleans. There, she studies creative writing, literature, and composition theory. She also works with ESL students in the UNO Writing Lab, where she helps them with revision. She wrote down her thoughts on revising for students using *The Multicultural Workshop.*

Finally, however, getting started means getting started. I can't recall how many times I've avoided even rereading the assignment. When I actually sit down and put some words on the page, my essay starts to take shape. If my cat could talk, I think he would tell me, "Go get some paper and a pen. Just start. Stop playing with me and get to it." And you know what? He'd be right.

—*Amanda Buege*

THE
MULTICULTURAL
WORKSHOP

BOOK 1

UNIT ONE
Identity

In this unit you will read four selections related to the theme of identity.

- What does the word *identity* mean to you?
- What are some
  of the ways we
  identify ourselves?

CHAPTER ONE

Who Are You?

1. **Pair work.** Get together with a partner. Take turns interviewing each other. Complete this chart with information about your partner.

Name _____

Age _____

Marital Status   ❑ Single   ❑ Married

Nationality _____

What languages do you speak?

_____

_____

What do you like to do?

_____

_____

_____

What organizations or groups did you belong to in the past?

_____

_____

_____

2. **Group work.** With your partner, get together with another pair of students. Use your chart to introduce your partner to them.

3. **Group work.** Read the information below and answer the question.

> In the poem on page 6, a student named Garett tells about himself in a letter to his history teacher, Miss Parsons. Garett writes to his teacher because he is failing history. What do you think he says in the letter? Make several predictions.

READING STRATEGY:
Predicting
See page 181.

_____

_____

_____

_____

_____

_____

_____

_____

_____

Read your predictions to the class.

4. **Class work.** Listen as your teacher reads the poem on the following page. Then read it aloud several times.

Garett Chandler
Period 3, Room 122

ABOUT THE AUTHOR
Mel Glenn is a teacher
and poet. Many of his
poems are written
from the point of view
of high-school stu-
dents in the United
States. This poem is
from a book called
Class Dismissed.

Miss Parsons, surely you jest.[1]
Me fail?
Don't you know who I am?
Let me refresh your memory.
I am
      captain of the quiz team,
      coordinator of the senior show,
      copy editor for the lit magazine.[2]
I am
      president of the debate club,
      point guard for the basketball team,
      peer tutor for the honor society.[3]
I am
      senior section editor for the yearbook,[4]
      student rep for homeroom, and
      salutatorian[5] for this year's class.
Miss Parsons, let's talk this over.
You can't fail me.
I don't have time to study history.
I'm making it instead.

— *Mel Glenn*

---

1 **jest**   joke
2 **lit magazine**   literary magazine; a school magazine of student writing
3 **honor society**   a group of students with high grades
4 **yearbook**   a book published by the senior class of a high school or college
5 **salutatorian**   the second-highest ranking student in a class

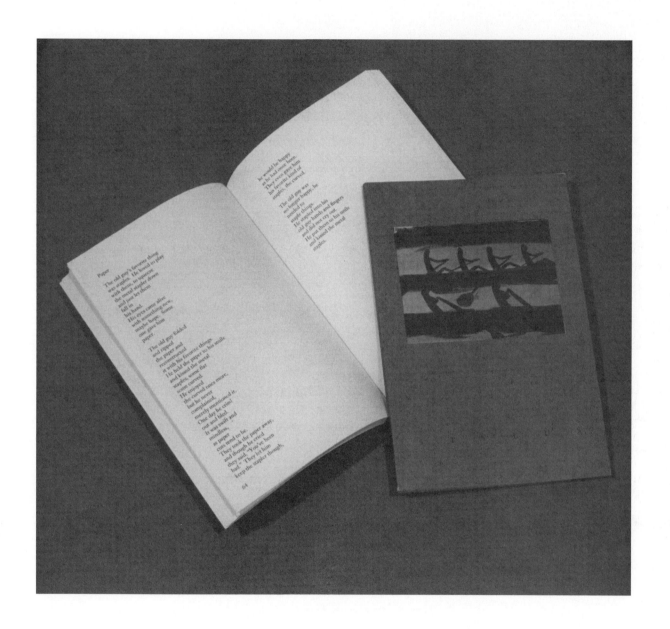

READING STRATEGY:
Making Inferences
See page 180.

5. **Class work.** In the poem, Garett identifies himself by listing his roles. What can you infer about Garett from these roles? List your ideas in the chart below.

Garett's Roles	What can you infer about Garett?
captain of the quiz team	He's smart.
copy editor of the lit magazine	He's a good writer.
president of the debate club	

What's your impression of Garett? Share ideas with your classmates and teacher.

6. **Journal writing.** How do you think Miss Parsons might respond to Garett? Write her response in a letter to Garett.

Keep these ideas in mind as you write in your journal:

• Use journal assignments to explore your own ideas.

• There are no right or wrong answers in journal assignments.

• Your journal writing will not be corrected.

Example:

Dear Mr. Chandler,

I appreciated receiving your note, and I enjoyed reading about your many accomplishments. While I can see....

Sincerely,
Miss Parsons

7. **Journal writing.** Make a chart like the one below. In the first column, list your roles, interests, and accomplishments. Ask a partner to complete the right side of your chart.

Example:

My Roles, Interests, and Accomplishments	What can you infer?
I'm a college student.	My partner is smart.
I like to travel.	He is adventurous.
I have a high-school diploma.	He's a good student.

8. **Writing Assignment.**

   a. On one sheet of paper, present yourself to your classmates—**without** using words. Instead of words, use photographs, drawings, or pictures cut from magazines.

   b. On another piece of paper, tell why you chose each picture. Explain what each picture tells about you.

   c. Show your pictures to a classmate. What does your classmate think the pictures tell about you?

   d. Make a class display of pictures. Try to match the pictures with your classmates.

   e. Place your papers in your writing folder.

CHAPTER TWO

What Do We Have in Common?

❉★❉★❉★❉★❉★❉★

WRITING STRATEGY:
Listing Ideas
See page 172.

1. **Pair Work.** What do you and your partner have in common? How are you alike? List your ideas.

   Examples: *We are both students.*

   We are both male/female.

   _____

   _____

   _____

   _____

   Which of your sentences are true for everyone in the class?

   Example: *We are all students.*

   _____

   _____

   Read these sentences to your classmates. See if they agree with you.

❉★❉★❉★❉★❉★❉★

READING STRATEGY:
Predicting
See page 181.

2. **Pair Work.** Read the title of the folk tale on page 12. What do you think a king and a poor boy might have in common? Suggest several possibilities.

   _____

   _____

   _____

   _____

   Compare predictions with your classmates.

3. **On Your Own.** Read the folk tale quickly to find words and phrases that describe the king and the boy. List them in the chart below.

READING STRATEGY:
Reading for Specific Information
See page 182.

Boy

grateful

_____

_____

_____

King

has all the power

_____

_____

_____

4. **Pair Work.** Compare charts from Activity 3. Show where in the story you found the words and phrases. Then compare ideas with your classmates.

5. **On Your Own.** In this folk tale, a king learns something from a poor boy. Read the folk tale again to find out what the king learns. Write your ideas below.

_____

_____

_____

The King and the Poor Boy

(A Cambodian Folk Tale)

In a small village near the edge of the forest, there once lived a boy who had no mother or father. His uncle, who was the chief cook for the king, pitied[1] the poor boy. So he invited the boy to stay with him in the palace. The grateful boy worked hard to help his uncle. He washed the plates, polished the cups, cleaned the dining room tables, and mopped the floors. At the end of each month, his uncle gave him six *sen* as his wages.

Now the king frequently inspected the palace quarters. He often noticed the hardworking boy mopping the floors or polishing the cups, cheerfully and in good humor. One day the king asked the boy, "Do you receive wages for your hard work?"

The boy bowed and said, "Yes, I do, Your Majesty. I earn six *sen* every month."

Then the king asked, "Do you think you are rich or do you think you are poor?"

---

1 **pitied**   felt sorry for

"Your Majesty," the boy replied, "I think that I am as rich as a king."

The king was taken by surprise. "Why is this poor boy talking such nonsense[2]?" he mused to himself.

Once more, the king spoke to the boy, "I am a king and I have all the power and riches of this country. You earn only six *sen* a month. Why do you say you are as rich as I am?"

The boy laid down his broom and slowly replied to the king, "Your Majesty, I may receive only six *sen* each month, but I eat from one plate and you also eat from one plate. I sleep for one night and you also sleep for one night. We eat and sleep the same. There is no difference. Now, Your Majesty, do you understand why I say that I am as rich as a king?"

The king understood and was satisfied.

---

2 **nonsense** foolishness

6. **Pair Work.** The actions of the king and the boy give information about their personalities. What inferences can you make about the king and the boy from these lines in the story?

⬛✦⬛✦⬛✦⬛

READING STRATEGY:
Making Inferences
See page 180.

a. His uncle, who was the chief cook for the king, pitied the poor boy. So he invited the boy to stay with him in the palace.

Inference: _The uncle was a kind man._____

b. The king frequently inspected the palace quarters.

Inference: _____

_____

_____

c. The boy bowed and said, "Yes, I do, Your Majesty."

Inference: _____

_____

_____

Read your inferences to your classmates and teacher.

7. **Journal Writing.** Imagine that you are the king in the folk tale. Reflect on your conversation with the boy. Here are some questions you might think about:

• What did the boy say to you? What does it mean to you?

• How did you feel after your conversation with the boy?

• What's your impression of the boy?

• Did you learn anything from the boy? If so, what?

8. **Writing Assignment.** In writing, tell your classmates about a quality or characteristic that two of your friends have in common. Read the ideas below for more specific suggestions.

   a. Choose two friends you know well.

   b. Think of qualities they have in common. (For example, are they both kind, generous, or energetic?) Make a list.

   c. Choose one quality from your list to write about.

   d. In writing, tell your classmates about this quality in your friends. Use details and examples to show this quality in your two friends.

   e. Read Around. Get together with a group of classmates. Take turns reading each other's writing.

   f. Place your writing in your writing folder.

CHAPTER THREE

What Do Actions Reveal?

❈✦❈✦❈✦❈✦❈

WRITING STRATEGY:
Making a Tree Diagram
See page 174.

1. Journal Writing. Think of a friend or relative. Make a diagram like the one below. List words and ideas to describe this person.

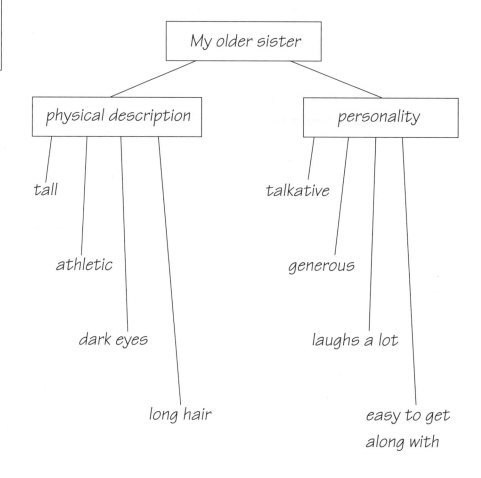

My older sister

physical description

personality

tall

athletic

dark eyes

long hair

talkative

generous

laughs a lot

easy to get along with

2. On Your Own. The story on the following pages describes the actions of two people in a difficult situation. Read the story and look for the information below.

READING STRATEGY:
Reading for Specific Information
See page 182.

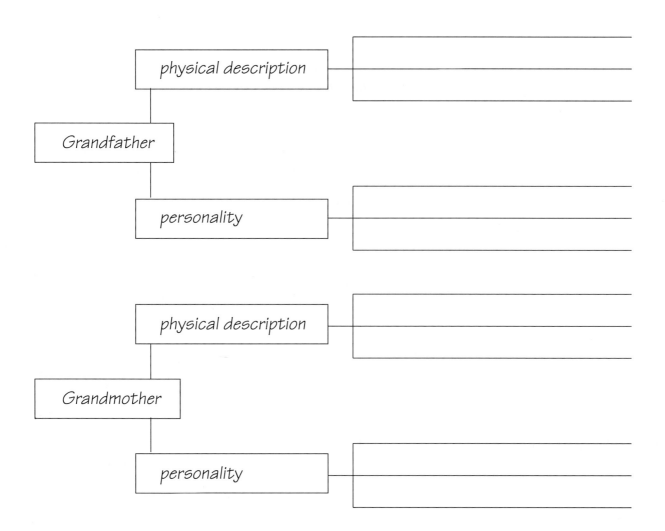

Compare charts with your classmates.

3. On Your Own. Read the story again.

from The Land I Lost

by Huynh Quang Nhuong

My grandmother had married a man whom she loved with all her heart, but who was totally different from her. My grandfather was very shy, never laughed loudly, and always spoke very softly. And physically he was not as strong as my grandmother. But he excused his lack of physical strength by saying that he was a "scholar."

About three months after their marriage, my grandparents were in a restaurant and a rascal[1] began to insult my grandfather because he looked weak and had a pretty wife. At first he just made insulting remarks, such as, "Hey! Wet chicken! This is no place for a weakling!"

My grandfather wanted to leave the restaurant even though he and my grandmother had not yet finished their meal. But my grandmother pulled his shirt sleeve and signaled him to remain seated. She continued to eat and looked as if nothing had happened.

Tired of yelling insults without any result, the rascal got up from his table, moved over to my grandparents' table, and grabbed my grandfather's chopsticks. My grandmother immediately wrested the chopsticks from him and struck the rascal on his cheekbone with her elbow. The blow was so quick and powerful that he lost his balance and fell on the floor….

ABOUT THE AUTHOR
Huynh Quang Nhuong was born in Mytho, Vietnam. He now lives in Columbia, Missouri. *The Land I Lost* is his first book.

---

1 **rascal**   a dishonest person

While the rascal's friends tried to revive him, everyone else surrounded my grandmother and asked her who had taught her karate.[2] She said, "Who else? My husband!"

After the fight at the restaurant people assumed[3] that my grandfather knew karate very well but refused to use it for fear of killing someone. In reality, my grandmother had received special training in karate from my great-great uncle from the time she was eight years old.

Anyway, after that incident, my grandfather never had to worry again. Anytime he had some business downtown, people treated him very well. And whenever anyone happened to bump into him on the street, they bowed to my grandfather in a very respectful way.

---

2 **karate**   a style of fighting, using hands and feet
3 **assumed**   believed something to be true without proof

READING STRATEGY:
Paraphrasing
See page 180.

READING STRATEGY:
Summarizing
See page 183.

4. **Pair Work.** Retell the story in your own words. Take turns giving information.

5. **On Your Own.** In the diagram below, summarize the story. Tell only the most important things that happened.

Story Plot (What Happened?)

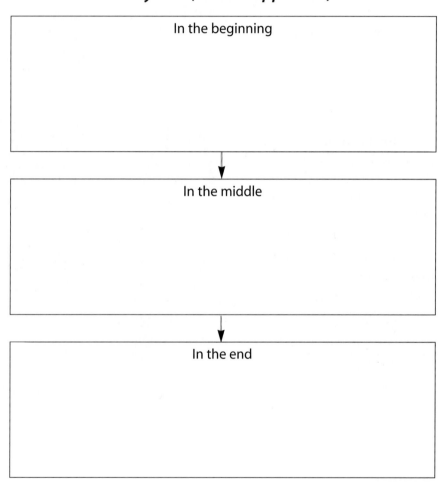

In the beginning

In the middle

In the end

Compare diagrams with your classmates.

6. **Pair Work.** The actions of the rascal, grandmother, and grandfather give information about their personalities. What do these lines from the story reveal about their personalities?

READING STRATEGY:
Making Inferences
See page 180.

a. *A rascal began to insult my grandfather because he looked weak and had a pretty wife. My grandfather wanted to leave the restaurant even though he and my grandmother had not yet finished their meal. But my grandmother pulled his shirt sleeve and signaled him to remain seated. She continued to eat and looked as if nothing had happened.*

Inferences about the rascal: *I think the rascal was aggressive.*

_____

Inferences about the grandmother: *I think the grandmother*

_____

Inferences about the grandfather: *I think the grandfather*

_____

b. *The rascal…grabbed my grandfather's chopsticks. My grandmother immediately wrested the chopsticks from him and struck the rascal on his cheekbone with her elbow. The blow was so quick and powerful that he lost his balance and fell on the floor.*

Inferences about the grandmother: _____

_____

Inferences about the grandfather: _____

_____

Read your inferences to your classmates.

WRITING STRATEGY:
Quickwriting
See page 176.

7. Writing Assignment. In writing, tell your classmates a story about a friend or relative. Here are some ideas to help you get started:

a. Think again about your friend or relative from Activity 1. In your journal, quickwrite for ten minutes about this person. Write down any memories of this person that come to mind. (When you quickwrite, you write as fast as you can. You do not pay attention to grammar or spelling. You try to get down as many thoughts as you can.)

b. Choose a memory from your quickwriting. Choose something that reveals your friend's or relative's personality.

c. Relate the memory in a story about this person.

d. Read Around. Get together with a group of classmates. Take turns reading each other's writing.

e. Place your writing in your writing folder.

CHAPTER FOUR

What Makes Up a Life Story?

1. **Class Work.** A biography is the story of another person's life. What important information might you include in a biography? Brainstorm ideas and write them on a cluster diagram on the board.

❋★❋★❋★❋★❋

WRITING STRATEGY:
Making a Cluster Diagram
See page 173.

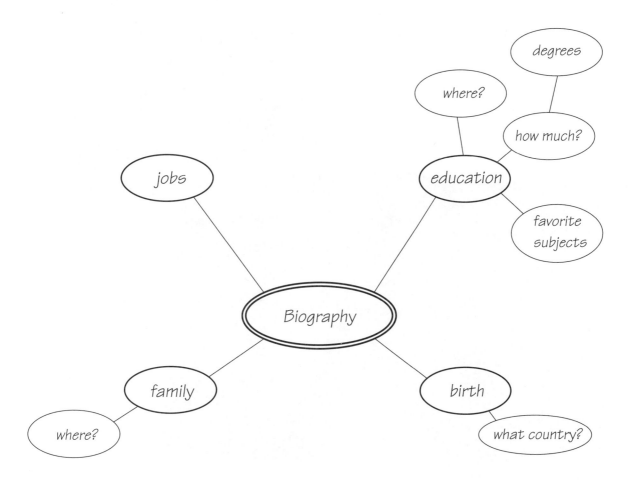

❋★❋★❋★❋

READING STRATEGY:
Asking Questions
See page 178.

2. **Class Work.** These pictures give information about An Wang.
   Study the pictures and read the time line of An Wang's life on page
   25. What questions do you have about him? Write them in the
   chart on page 25.

Time Line of An Wang's Life	Your Questions	Answers
1945 left China and came to the United States	*Why did he leave China?*	
1948 earned a Ph.D.		
1950 invented the "magnetic core"		
1951 started his own business		
1985 his company earned $2 billion		

3. **On Your Own.** On the following pages, read about An Wang and look for answers to your questions. Next to your questions in the chart above, write any answers you find.

READING STRATEGY:
Reading for Specific Information
See page 182.

Without Hesitation
A Biography of An Wang

An Wang came to the United States in 1945. In 1986, he was one of twelve immigrants to receive a Liberty Medal from the President of the United States. Dr. Wang died in 1990.

1   On his way home from school one day, An Wang found a bird's nest that had fallen from a tree. Inside the nest was a baby sparrow. Wang picked up the nest and took it home with him. He was a little nervous about showing the bird to his parents, so he decided to leave it outside for a while. When he finally went outside to get the bird, it was gone. "It was my first lesson in the importance of acting rather than hesitating," Wang wrote many years later. It was a lesson that stayed with Wang for his entire life.

2   When An Wang came to the United States in 1945, he had already lost both of his parents and one sister. He had also lived through a civil war[1] in China. But these troubles taught him an important lesson. By the time he left China, he believed that he could try to accomplish anything; nothing was impossible.

3   In 1948, only three years after arriving in the United States, Wang earned a Ph.D.[2] in Physics from Harvard University. After he got his Ph.D., he stayed at Harvard and worked in the Computation Laboratory. It was at this time that he invented the magnetic core. This device was a basic part of computer memory until the use of microchips in the late 1960s.

4   In 1951 Wang decided that he was tired of working for other people. With his savings of $600 he started his own company, Wang Laboratories. His first office had a table, chair, and telephone— nothing more.

---

1 **civil war**   a war between groups of people inside one country
2 **Ph.D.**   an abbreviation for Doctor of Philosophy, an advanced university degree

5   The business grew steadily. At first Wang sold electronic components.[3] Later he designed and sold calculators. And he didn't forget what he had learned about hesitating. When it was time to change the company's direction, he acted. When it was time to leave a market, he didn't hesitate. In the late 1960s he realized that Japanese companies would soon control the calculator market. Wang Laboratories went on to other things, including the personal computer. In 1985, sales for the company reached $2 billion.

6   Success didn't change Wang's lifestyle very much. Before he became the owner of a highly successful business, he lived simply with his wife and three children. Years later, when he was worth more than $1 billion, he still owned only two suits. And he lived in a house that many people thought was too simple for a successful businessman.

7   In his autobiography, Wang expressed his belief that "both individuals and corporations[4] have the responsibility to make some positive contribution to the world." Dr. Wang acted on this belief many times by supporting programs for the arts, education, and medical care in the city of Boston. And perhaps more importantly, he showed that a person could be successful in business without sacrificing personal values.

---

3 **components**   parts of a machine
4 **corporations**   large business organizations

4. **Pair Work.** Compare answers to your questions in Activity 2. Show where in the text you found the answers. Then share your questions and answers with your classmates.

5. **Journal Writing.** In your own words, write about An Wang's life. Use the time line on page 25 for information.

6. **On Your Own.** These sentences are from An Wang's biography. Use context—the other words in the sentences—to help you guess the meaning of each **boldfaced** word. Then compare guesses with your classmates.

a. *On his way home from school one day, An Wang found a bird's* **nest** *that had fallen from the tree. Inside the nest was a baby sparrow.*

My guess: _____

_____

_____

b. *It was at this time that he invented the* **magnetic core**. *This device was a basic part of computer memory until the use of microchips in the late 1960s.*

My guess: _____

_____

_____

c. *In 1951 Wang decided that he was* **tired of** *working for other people. With his savings of $600 he started his own company, Wang Laboratories.*

My guess: _____

_____

_____

❋ ❤ ❋ ❤ ❋ ❤ ❋ ❤ ❋

READING STRATEGY:
Paraphrasing
See page 180.

READING STRATEGY:
Using Context
See page 184.

d. *Success didn't change Wang's **lifestyle** very much. Before he became the owner of a highly successful business, he lived simply with his wife and children. Years later, when he was worth more than $1 billion, he still owned only two suits.*

My guess: _____

_____

_____

e. *In his autobiography, Wang expressed the belief that "both individuals and corporations have the responsibility to make some positive **contribution** to the world." Dr. Wang acted on this belief many times by supporting programs for the arts, education, and medical care in the city of Boston.*

My guess: _____

_____

_____

7. Group Work. Follow the instructions below.

a. The first paragraph of a piece of writing is sometimes called a "hook." Like a hook to catch fish, a hook in writing catches readers and pulls them into the story. Ask your teacher to read aloud the first sentence of An Wang's biography. Without looking at the biography, work together to retell the rest of the paragraph in your own words.

b. In your group, evaluate the first paragraph. Do you think it is an effective hook? Why or why not? Choose one person to report your group's answer to the class.

CRITICAL THINKING STRATEGY:
Evaluating
See page 189.

CRITICAL THINKING STRATEGY:
Classifying
See page 187.

8. **Group Work.** What kinds of information did the writer include about An Wang? Check these items in the list below. Then write the number of the paragraph with the information.

Checklist

Year of Birth	❑	*paragraph* _____
Country of Birth	❑	*paragraph* _____
Education	✓	*paragraph* __3__
Family Relationships	❑	*paragraph* _____
Accomplishments	❑	*paragraph* _____
Important Events	❑	*paragraph* _____
Values	❑	*paragraph* _____
Anecdotes	❑	*paragraph* _____
Lifestyle	❑	*paragraph* _____

Compare this list with your ideas in Activity 1. What's the same? What's different? Talk it over with your classmates.

9. **Writing Assignment.** Write a biography of someone in your class. Here are some steps you can follow:

   a. On Your Own. Make a time line of important events in your life.

   b. Pair Work. Exchange time lines with a partner. Read your partner's time line and ask questions to get more information. Take notes on your partner's answers.

   c. Use the time line and your notes to write your partner's biography. Think of an interesting "hook" to begin the biography.

   d. Read Around. Get together with a group of classmates. Take turns reading each other's writing.

   e. Place your writing in your writing folder.

U N I T   O N E
Final Project

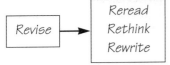

Revise	→	Reread Rethink Rewrite

You should now have four pieces of work in your writing folder, one from the writing assignment at the end of each chapter. Each of the pieces in your writing folder is called a first draft. A first draft is a rough copy—a collection of first ideas.

Your final project is to revise one of your first drafts. Your revised writing will then be collected in a booklet for your classmates to read. Your teacher will also use your revised writing to help you evaluate your progress.

Many writers say that revising is the most important stage in writing. As you revise your writing, you work to make it clearer, more complete, and more forceful. You might add information, take out information, and move things around. You might revise your writing one time or many times.

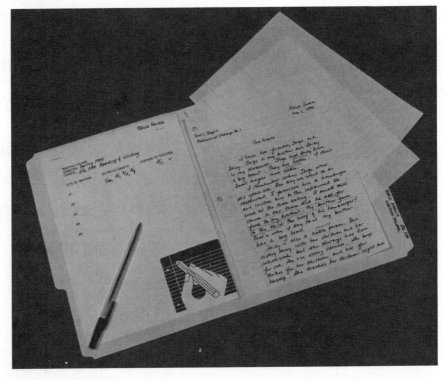

There are no simple steps to follow as you revise your writing. However, there are a number of revising strategies you can try:

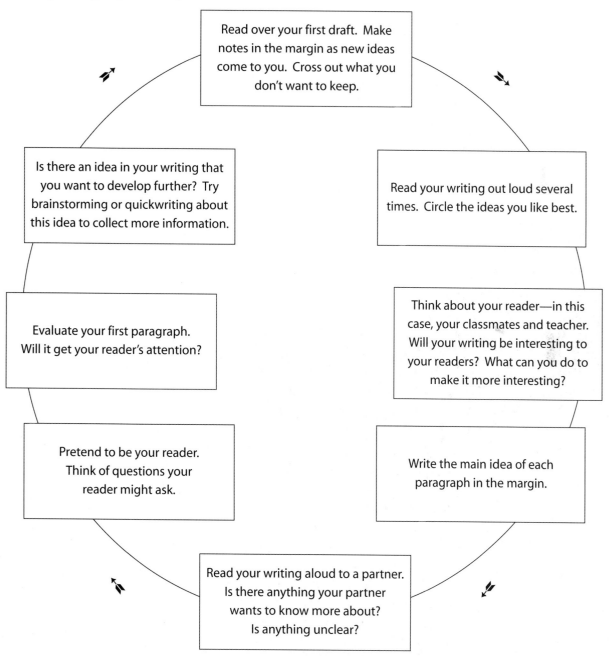

Read over your first draft. Make notes in the margin as new ideas come to you. Cross out what you don't want to keep.

Read your writing out loud several times. Circle the ideas you like best.

Is there an idea in your writing that you want to develop further? Try brainstorming or quickwriting about this idea to collect more information.

Think about your reader—in this case, your classmates and teacher. Will your writing be interesting to your readers? What can you do to make it more interesting?

Evaluate your first paragraph. Will it get your reader's attention?

Write the main idea of each paragraph in the margin.

Pretend to be your reader. Think of questions your reader might ask.

Read your writing aloud to a partner. Is there anything your partner wants to know more about? Is anything unclear?

Before you start revising your own paper, look over the next four pages. On pages 34–35, you can see how one writer revised her paper. On page 36–37, you can read another writer's ideas about revising.

Read these drafts to see how one writer revised her writing.

First Draft

My name is Maria A. Castro. I was born in Rivas, Nicaragua, in December, 1953. I have five brothers and one sister. My father died four years ago, and my mother lives with my sister in Honduras.

Fourteen years ago, my family and I left Nicaragua because a civil war hit the country. The new regime forced many Nicaraguans to flee. I lived in Honduras during eight years. Now I am living in New Orleans, Louisiana, with my husband and my children.

In 1988, when we moved to the United States, the situation was very hard. We began a new life and a new home, but the language and the culture was a barrier that we had to overcome. Now all is different. My husband has a good work, my daughter finished high school, my son will finish high school in two years, and I am studying English at Delgado. I hope to get a good work when my English is better.

I like to keep my house clean and in order. I think I am a good wife and a good mother. In my free time, I like to sew and read. This is a relax for me.

Note: Maria A. Castro is a student in Betty Speyrer's ESL class at Delgado Community College, New Orleans, Louisiana. She wrote these drafts in Ms. Speyrer's reading-writing class.

Third Draft

My name is Maria A. Castro. I was born in Rivas, Nicaragua, Central America, in December, 1953. I have five brothers and one sister. My father died four years ago, and my mother lives with my sister in Honduras.

When I was a child, I had many friends, and I enjoyed being with them. All the time, we ran and jumped. I always remember that time because it was the best time in my life.

Fourteen years ago, I was a hospital secretary in Rivas. My father was my boss. We were a happy family, but we left our country because a civil war broke out. Many Nicaraguans fled because of political persecution. My family fled to Honduras. In Honduras, I met my husband, and we were married on December 12, 1986.

In January, 1988, my husband and I decided to come to the United States because we wanted a better education for our children. Beginning a new life was very hard for us. We learned to overcome our fear of the new language and the new culture.

Now all is different. My husband has a good job, my daughter has finished high school, my son will finish high school in two years, and I am studying English at Delgado. I am very happy living in the United States.

In my house, I am very responsible. I like to be a good wife and a good mother. I like to cook all kinds of food, especially Nicaraguan food. In my free time, I like to sew and to read. This is relaxing for me.

New information about the writer's childhood

More complete information about the writer's family

New detail about the writer's husband

New reason for moving to the United States

New opinion

*New opinion
New detail*

One Writer's Thoughts on Revising

Revise: Rewrite
Rethink
Review

I always try to remember that revision means *rewriting*, not just fixing a word here and there. Revising an essay can actually mean *rethinking* an essay. It also means looking at the writing with fresh eyes *(revision)*.

Read your writing out loud.

I like to read my writing out loud. I can't praise oral reading enough! So many times, I *hear* problems that I don't see. My boyfriend is patient. Usually, I can enlist him to be my listener. When at school, I'll catch a friend or classmate and read aloud a paragraph or section that I'm feeling uncomfortable about.

Check for details.

Even on first drafts, I allow myself enough time to revise. I always, *always*, wait until the next day. This gives me some perspective. Then, I divide up the job so that it doesn't seem enormous. I read the first time through (out loud) to check for little errors, although this is not the most important part of revising. Grammar errors are the easiest to hear. If a sentence sounds wrong, I make a mark in the margin. I'll come back later to check it over.

Check for important ideas.

The second time through, I listen to make sure that each paragraph discusses one main idea. Sometimes, I write the main idea of each paragraph in the margin. If I can't do this quickly or easily, I know I have some real rewriting to do.

Pretend to be your reader.

The third time through, I pretend to be someone else. I play "devil's advocate"[1] with my own writing. "What does Amanda mean here?" I ask myself. "She's not being very clear." Or "Well

---

1 **play devil's advocate**   take the opposite position; look at something from the opposite point of view

now, how in the world does this idea relate to what Amanda was just talking about?" Reading my writing from a different point of view helps me a lot.

If I'm lucky, I'll only need to write two or three drafts before the writing feels right. Other days, other weeks, other months, I know I'll be finished after five or even ten drafts! "Revise, revise, revise," is the writer's motto. It's almost identical to the musician's motto, "Practice, practice, practice."

—Amanda Buege

Revise, revise, revise.

ABOUT THE AUTHOR
Amanda Buege is a graduate student at the University of New Orleans. There, she studies creative writing, literature, and composition theory. She also works with ESL students in the UNO Writing Lab, where she helps them with revision. She wrote down her thoughts on revising for students using *The Multicultural Workshop.*

UNIT TWO
Change

In this unit you will read four selections related to the theme of change.

- Think of something that changes over time.
- Tell how it changes.

CHAPTER ONE

Growing Up

WRITING STRATEGY:
Listing Ideas
See page 172.

1. **Class Work.** How do children change as they grow up, or become adults? List your ideas on the board or below.

Growing Up

They get taller.

They become more responsible.

2. **Journal Writing.** Describe yourself at the age of ten. Write at least five sentences.

WRITING STRATEGY: *Providing Details* See page 176.

Example:

I was very shy.

I was tall for my age.

I had a lot of friends.

I lived with my family.

I liked to do things outdoors.

Describe yourself today. Tell how you have changed or stayed the same.

Example:

I am still very shy.

I am not tall.

I have a lot of friends.

I don't live with my family now.

I like to do things outdoors.

3. **Pair Work.** Read each other's sentences from Activity 2. Look for one way your partner has changed. Tell the class about the change.

Example:

When my partner was ten years old, she lived with her family. Now she doesn't live with her family.

4. **Class Work.** The following poem tells about the changes in one person's life. Listen as your teacher reads the poem aloud.

Yesterday

✳ ✦ ✳ ✦ ✳ ✦ ✳ ✳

ABOUT THE AUTHOR
Jean Little was born in
Taiwan in 1932. She
later became a poet
and a teacher of
handicapped children.
This selection is from a
collection of her
poems entitled
Hey World, Here I Am!

Yesterday I knew all the answers
Or I knew my parents did.

Yesterday I had my Best Friend
And my Second Best Friend
And I knew whose Best Friend I was
And who disliked me.

Yesterday I hated asparagus and coconut and parsnips
And mustard pickles and olives
And anything I'd never tasted.

Yesterday I knew what was Right and what was Wrong
And I never had any trouble deciding which was which.
It always seemed so obvious.[1]

But today…everything's changing.
I suddenly have a million unanswered questions.
Everybody I meet might become a friend.
I tried eating snails with garlic sauce—and I liked them!
And I know the delicate[2] shadings[3] that lie between
Good and evil—and I face their dilemma.[4]
Life is harder now…and yet, easier…
And more and more exciting!

—*Jean Little*

---

1 **obvious**   easy to understand
2 **delicate**   not easy to recognize
3 **shadings**   small differences in degree
4 **dilemma**   a difficult choice

5. Pair Work. Together read the poem on pages 42–43 aloud. Then choose a way to divide the poem so that each of you reads a different part.

6. Pair Work. Read the poem again. What changes does the speaker in the poem mention? List them in the chart below. Then compare charts with your classmates.

READING STRATEGY:
*Taking Notes
in a Chart*
See page 183.

Yesterday	Today
She knew all the answers.	*She doesn't know all the answers.*

**CRITICAL THINKING
STRATEGY:**
Interpreting
See page 190.

7. Class Work. What's your reaction to the poem? Here are some questions you might talk about:

• The speaker in the poem first describes herself as a child. Do you think she was a typical child? Why or why not?

• What do you think is the most important way she has changed? Why?

• What do you think she means in the last two lines of the poem? Do you agree?

8. On Your Own. Tell about yourself as a child and as an adult. Complete these sentences. Then compare responses with a classmate.

When I was a child,

a. I liked to _____

_____

b. I didn't like to _____

_____

c. I had trouble _____

_____

d. I didn't have trouble _____

_____

Now

a. I like to _____

_____

b. I don't like to _____

_____

c. I have trouble _____

_____

d. I never have trouble _____

_____

9. **Journal Writing.** What changes would you include in a poem about yourself? List several ideas. Read them to a classmate.

Example:

Yesterday

  I didn't like to try new things.

  I never disagreed with anyone.

  I worried about how I looked.

Today

  I like to try new things.

  I have strong opinions about lots of things.

  I don't worry about how I look.

10. **Writing Assignment.**

    a. Take out two blank pages of paper. Label one page "Yesterday" and one page "Today."

    b. On the "Yesterday" page, present yourself to your classmates as you were in the past. On the "Today" page, present yourself as you are now. Use these ideas or think of your own:

       • Write words, phrases, and/or sentences.

       • Use words cut from magazines or newspapers.

       • Use drawings, symbols, or photographs.

    c. Read Around. Get together with several classmates. Take turns reading each other's papers.

    d. Place your writing in your writing folder.

CHAPTER TWO

Growing Old

1. Group Work. Brainstorm answers to the question below. Choose one person to report your group's answers to the class.

In your opinion, when is a person "old"?

❊ ✔ ❊ ✔ ❊ ✔ ❊

WRITING STRATEGY:
Brainstorming
See page 169.

❊ ✔ ❊ ✔ ❊ ✔ ❊

**CRITICAL THINKING
STRATEGY:**
Evaluating
See page 189.

2. Group Work. List the advantages and disadvantages of old age. Then add your ideas to a class list on the board.

Advantages	Disadvantages
+	−
_____	_____
_____	_____
_____	_____

3. On Your Own. Read the dialogues on the following pages to find out what these people have to say about old age.

from Old Is What You Get

Dialogues on Aging by the Old and Young
by Ann Zane Shanks

Mimi Martin, Age 88

I don't feel old, but my eyes, ears, and legs tell me I am. I had a big library, over one hundred books, but I can't read any more. My mind works all the time. When you get old, you lose your independence. But I'm lucky, my children and grandchildren are very nice to me.

Dr. Louis Kushner, Age 87

Now that I'm an older age, I'm reading much more and understanding much more. I can truthfully say that I am more aware of life today. I feel people more. There is a new humanitarian aspect in me. I'm beginning to feel sorry for people I was too busy to pay attention to before.

Frederic H. Stephens, Age 96

You have to admit when you grow older that you also grow better. Better, because you have time to ponder and forget your sins of omission. They are in the past. I don't scold my wife as much as I used to, and she doesn't scold me as much as she used to. She'd scold me because I

didn't take my nap. I admit she did it because she loved me and wanted me to take care of myself. And I'd scold her because she did too much work. I'd do it probably for the same reason. In this day and age Arline and I get along very nicely.

Hope Bagger, Age 84

I usually do feel well and my eyes don't bother me so often. The only thing that bothers me is that I can't read in bed because I have to take my glasses off and nowadays I need two magnifying glasses in order to read. I can't see your face at all. I take things as they come. Every age has its advantages. People at eighty-three are just about the same people as they were when they were forty-three or twenty-three or whatever. So you have advantages at every season. I used to be ill more of the time than I am nowadays. I used to get bronchitis because I didn't give in to a cold. I used to get a lot of headaches, too, but not any more.

4. Pair Work. List examples from the reading.

Advantages of Old Age +	Disadvantages of Old Age −
_____	_____
_____	_____
_____	_____
_____	_____

How is this list different from your list in Activity 2? Compare ideas with your classmates.

WRITING STRATEGY:
Giving Examples
See page 171.

5. Pair Work. Think of examples to illustrate these lines from the reading:

a. *When you get old, you lose your independence.*

Example:

Many older people have to stop driving. They have to depend

on other people to take them places.

_____

_____

b. *I don't feel old, but my eyes, ears, and legs tell me I am.*

_____

_____

c. *You have to admit when you grow older that you also grow better.*

_____

_____

d. *Every age has its advantages.*

_____

_____

Read your examples to your classmates.

6. Class Work.

WRITING STRATEGY:
Brainstorming
See page 169.

a. Brainstorm a set of words and phrases to describe the people pictured below. Write your ideas on the board.

b. Imagine you are one of the people above. Write a sentence telling something about yourself. Read your sentence to the class.

7. Journal Writing. Imagine yourself at the age of ninety. Describe your life at this age. Here are some questions you might think about:

• How do you feel?

• How do you spend your days?

• What problems, if any, do you have?

Tell a classmate how you imagine yourself at ninety.

8. **Writing Assignment.** In writing, tell your classmates about an older person you know well. Here are some suggestions to help you get started:

   a. Think about an older person you know well. Choose words and ideas to describe him or her. Add them to a diagram like this:

   Example:

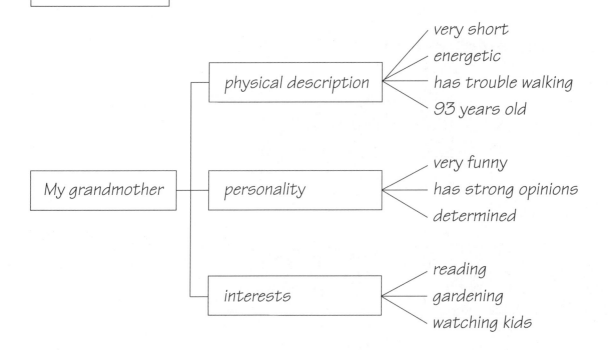

CRITICAL THINKING STRATEGY: *Classifying*
See page 187.

   b. In your journal, quickwrite about this person for ten minutes. Write down anything that comes to mind.

   c. Tell a classmate about this person. Answer any questions your classmate has.

   d. In writing, describe this person to your classmates.

   e. Read Around. Get together with a group of classmates. Take turns reading each other's writing.

   f. Place your writing in your writing folder.

WRITING STRATEGY: *Quickwriting*
See page 176.

CHAPTER THREE

Changing the Way You Live

1. Journal Writing.

a. Describe the way you live now. Quickwrite in your journal for five minutes. Here are some questions you can use to get started:

WRITING STRATEGY:
Quickwriting
See page 176.

- Where do you live now? Why are you living there?

- What do you like about living there? What do you dislike?

- What makes your life difficult? What makes it easy?

- What in your life makes you happy? What makes you unhappy?

b. Imagine yourself in ten years. Describe the way you will live.

2. Pair Work. Tell your partner how your life might change over the next ten years. Use ideas from your journal writing in Activity 1.

3. Pair Work. Read the information below. With your partner, make a prediction.

READING STRATEGY:
Predicting
See page 181.

Folk tales exist in every culture. These stories are told by adults to children who tell them to their own children. Some folk tales give important lessons for living happily or successfully.

The title of the folk tale on the next page is very strange —it's a kind of riddle. Read the title and the first paragraph of the folk tale. What do you think the title might mean? Write your ideas.

_____

_____

_____

Compare ideas with your classmates.

4. Class Work. Read the folk tale on the following pages and check your prediction from Activity 3.

Don't Throw Stones from "Not Yours" to "Yours"

(An Israeli Folk Tale)

There was once a rich man with a large house and beautiful gardens. He had many servants, and they constantly worked at beautifying his estate. As they worked in the gardens, they dug up many stones. The rich man ordered them to throw every stone over the wall into the road. Every day it was this way. The servants threw all of the stones over the wall into the road where people walked.

One day the rich man was standing at the gate while his workmen were throwing stones over the wall. An old man of the nearby village was passing. He stopped and protested to the rich man.

"Why do you throw stones from 'not yours' to 'yours'?" he asked.

"What are you talking about?" the rich man said. "I own this great house and the gardens around it. My land extends to this wall. The road on the other side has nothing to do with me."

The old villager shook his head.

"God has been very good to you, but you have forgotten that nothing in life is permanent,[1]" the villager said. And he went away, leaving the rich man to ponder his words. But the rich man did not ponder long. Soon he was walking among his workmen, telling them to throw more stones over the wall.

The years passed. The gardens were cleared of stones. And somehow the rich man's fortunes began to change. Little by little he lost his wealth. A time came when he had to sell a little of his beautiful gardens. Again he had to sell, and again. At last he gave up the house itself. He became shabby and poor. He was no better off than the most unfortunate and miserable of beggars.[2]

Then one day, when he was old, he walked along the road past the great estate that had once been his. As he walked, he stumbled among the stones on the road. His feet were bare, and the stones cut them and bruised them.

He stopped near the wall to rest his sore feet. And then he recalled the words of the villager who had said long ago, "Why do you throw stones from 'not yours' to 'yours'?"

---

1 **permanent** lasting forever
2 **beggars** people who have no money

READING STRATEGY:
Scanning
See page 182.

5. On Your Own. Scan the story on page 55. Find words that "paint a picture" of the man's life at the beginning and end of the story.

Beginning	End
rich	*shabby*
servants	

Compare lists with your classmates.

6. Pair Work. Choose five words from the list below. Use the words to write your own sentences about the story. Make some of your sentences true and some of them false. Write your sentences on another piece of paper.

Examples: *At the beginning of the story, the man had many servants. (T)*
The man wanted to build a wall around his house. (F)

servants	stones	protest
wall	road	permanent
change	sell	poor
beggar	sore	village

Read your sentences to your classmates. Ask them if the sentences are true or false.

7. **On Your Own.** In the story, the man's life changed gradually. In the diagram below, describe the man's life at different periods.

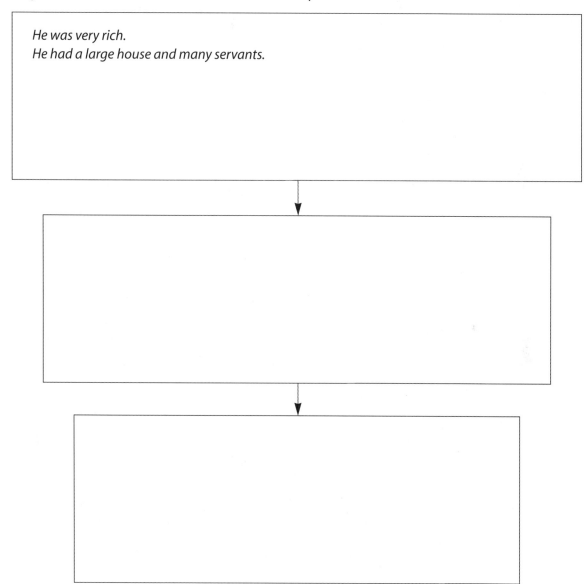

He was very rich.
He had a large house and many servants.

Exchange diagrams with a partner and compare ideas.

8. **Group Work.** Create a scene during one period in the man's life. Then act out the scene for the class.

9. **Journal Writing.** Choose one of the projects below. When you have finished writing, read your ideas to a classmate.

   • Rewrite the story in your own words.

   • Change one part of the story and rewrite that part.

   • Write a dialogue between two characters in the story.

   • Tell a folk tale that illustrates something about change.

WRITING STRATEGY:
Giving Examples
See page 171.

10. **On Your Own.** Read these sentences about the story. For each sentence, think of an example to support it—to show that it is true. Compare examples with a classmate.

   a. At the beginning of the story, the man was very rich.

      Example: *He had many servants.*

      _____

      _____

   b. The rich man was not very considerate.

      _____

      _____

   c. The rich man's lifestyle changed.

      _____

      _____

   d. At the end of the story the man was no longer rich.

      _____

      _____

11. **Writing Assignment.** In writing, describe an event that caused you to change in some way. Here are some suggestions to help you get started:

a. Make a list of important events in your life—things that caused you to change in some way.

   Example: • *My grandfather died.*
   • *I went to college.*
   • *I moved to New York.*

b. Choose one of the events on your list. Write it in the center of a cluster diagram. Then write down your thoughts about this event.

   Example:

❋ ★ ❋ ★ ❋ ★ ❋ ★ ❋

WRITING STRATEGY:
*Making a
Cluster Diagram*
See page 173.

no more visits after school

missed his jokes   no place to go in summer

felt lonely

shocked, sad, cried   made me think about death

My grandfather died.

life is short

realized I wasn't a child anymore   use time wisely

make my own decisions   need to be more responsible   appreciate people now

school   job

c. Tell a classmate about the event. Answer any questions your classmate has about the event.

d. In writing, describe this event to your classmates. Tell how it changed your life.

e. Exchange papers with a partner. Read your partner's writing.

f. Place your writing in your writing folder.

CHAPTER FOUR

Changing Where You Live

WRITING STRATEGY:
Making a Time Line
See page 174.

1. **Journal Writing.** Make a time line showing where you have lived and when. (Look at the example below.) On the left, write the year in which you were born and the place. Then add other places where you have lived. Write the year that you moved to each place.

   Example:

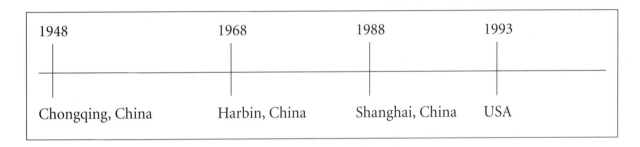

1948	1968	1988	1993
Chongqing, China	Harbin, China	Shanghai, China	USA

2. **Pair Work.** Exchange time lines. Choose one place on your partner's time line. Ask your partner questions about the move. Ask questions that begin with *Who, What, When, Where, Why,* or *How.*

   Examples: *Why did you move to Harbin?*
   What was difficult about the move?

   Tell your classmates what you learned about your partner.

3. **Pair Work.** Read the title and the first paragraph of the story on pages 62–63. What questions come to mind? Write them below.

READING STRATEGY:
Asking Questions
See page 178.

Question: _____*Why did she leave Russia?*_____

Prediction: _____

_____

Text answer: _____

_____

Question: _____

_____

Prediction: _____

_____

Text answer: _____

_____

Question: _____

_____

Prediction: _____

_____

Text answer: _____

_____

Read your questions to the class. Together predict answers.

4. **On Your Own.** Read the following essay to find answers to your questions.

From Russia to America in 1980

by Alla Pruzhansky

Immigrating from Russia does not mean that you sit on an airplane and the next day you arrive in America. It was a very long and painful trip.

In my school, many Russian children teased me because I was a Jew. In Russia, I was considered Jewish, not Russian. There were only three Jews in my class. Sometimes after school the children would hide, and when I came out with my friend, Diana (she was Jewish and kind of fat), they would come out and hit us, or say, "You are Jewish. Get out of here! We hate you! Go to your stupid Israel!" The Jewish boy in my class was very quiet because he was afraid of being hit and afraid of losing his friendship with Russian boys.

One day in 1980, my mother said, "I'm very tired of all of this." My father was against leaving. He had a lot of friends and a good job. The only reason my father wanted to leave was for me and my older sister.

My mother and father had to give up their jobs before they requested permission

to emigrate. We waited for the government's answer for four months and ten days. Finally we received it: "Yes."

We were not allowed to remain in our apartment, so we moved in with relatives. On June 6, 1980, my father, mother, sister, and I flew to a train station called Chop. A woman came up to me. She seemed kind and asked my name, my age, and grade in school. Then she said,

"Outside of Russia you will be given chewing gum with a drug that will make you very sick. You will never go to school. You will die from hunger." I was very scared, but my mother put me back in a good mood by explaining that the woman only wanted to scare me.

When we got on the train to go to Vienna, Austria, where all immigrants from Russia stop first, all of the bad things were forgotten. We remembered only the happy times in Russia. In Vienna, we had our choice: We could go to Israel or to another country. We said that we wanted to go to America to be with relatives.

Seven days later we went to Rome, where an American Jewish organization helped us. We filled out the application to go to the United States and every day for five months we waited for an answer.

On November 20, 1980, we flew on an airplane to New York. The flight was nine hours. People from an American Jewish organization met us and gave us money for food. I bought my first hot dog! That same day we flew to St. Louis, Missouri. At the airport, our friends were waiting for us. When we saw them, we were so happy that we cried. We had thought we would never see them again. It was like a dream. Finally our immigration was over. We were in the United States. This was a new world for us.

But here I discovered other problems. First, we went to school to learn English. After two months, I started sixth grade. There were so many children and they were so loud. Here in America they teased me because I came from Russia. But later on, they became my friends, and now I have a lot of friends.

My immigration was the most incredible thing that ever happened to me.

ABOUT THE AUTHOR
Alla Pruzhansky was eleven years old in 1980 when her family immigrated to the United States. Her story is not typical of every immigrant to America, but it does show some of the ways moving to a new place can be difficult and frightening.

5. Pair Work. Go back to your questions in Activity 3. Write any answers you found.

Write your unanswered questions on the board. Can your classmates find answers to these questions?

READING STRATEGY:
Using Context
See page 184.

6. Group Work. Find these words in the reading. Use the words and ideas around each new word (the context) to guess its meaning. Then check your guess by looking in a dictionary.

a. Paragraph 2: *teased*

My guess: _____

Dictionary definition: _____

b. Paragraph 2: *hide*

My guess: _____

Dictionary definition: _____

c. Paragraph 4: *give up*

My guess: _____

Dictionary definition: _____

d. Paragraph 5: *scare*

My guess: _____

Dictionary definition: _____

e. Paragraph 7: *filled out*

My guess: _____

Dictionary definition: _____

Compare answers with your classmates.

7. **Group Work.** Look back at the reading. What problems did Alla Pruzhansky have? List them. Then compare ideas with another group.

_____

_____

_____

_____

8. **Journal Writing.** Choose one move from your time line in Activity 1. What problems did this move cause for you? List them in your journal.

9. **Group Work.** Collect ideas about moving to a new place. List your group's ideas below.

> **WRITING STRATEGY:**
> *Collecting Information*
> See page 170.

Moving to a New Place

What problems did you and your classmates have? _____

_____

What was surprising about the new place? _____

_____

What was disappointing? _____

_____

What was easy to do? _____

_____

What was difficult to do? _____

_____

Choose someone to report your group's answer to one of the questions.

WRITING STRATEGY:
Understanding Your Audience
See page 177.

10. **Writing Assignment.** Write a letter to a friend in your native country. In your letter, urge your friend to visit you here. Here are some steps you can follow to help you get started:

a. Think of questions your friend might have about visiting you here. List these questions in your journal. Then write answers to these questions.

> **Example:** *How much money will I need?*
> *You won't need any money. I will pay for everything.*

b. Think of reasons your friend might give for not coming. List them in your journal. Then respond to these reasons.

> **Example:** *I'm too busy.*
> *I know you are busy, but I will only be here for a year.*

c. Write your letter, using ideas from your journal.

d. Read your letter to a classmate. Listen to your classmate's letter.

e. Place your letter in your writing folder.

UNIT TWO
Final Project

In your writing folder, you now have four pieces of writing for Unit 2, one from the writing assignment at the end of each chapter. Each piece of writing is a rough draft—a collection of first ideas.

For your final project, choose one of your rough drafts to revise. Your revised writing will then be collected and placed in a booklet for your classmates to read. Your teacher will also use your revised writing to help you evaluate your progress.

Although there are no simple steps to follow as you revise, you might try some of these strategies:

| Revise | → | Reread Rethink Rewrite |

Strategies

- Read over your first draft. Make notes in the margin as new ideas come to you. Cross out what you don't want to keep.

- Read your writing out loud several times. Circle the ideas you like best.

- Think about your reader—in this case, your classmates and teacher. Will your writing be interesting to your readers? What can you do to make it more interesting?

- Write the main idea of each paragraph in the margin.

- Read your writing aloud to a partner. Is there anything your partner wants to know more about? Is anything unclear?

- Pretend to be your reader. Think of questions your reader might ask.

- Evaluate your first paragraph. Will it get your reader's attention?

- Is there an idea in your writing that you want to develop further? Try brainstorming or quickwriting about this idea to collect more information.

As you revise, try to place yourself in your reader's shoes. Remember that your reader cannot read your mind. Your reader understands only as much as you explain on paper. Ask yourself these questions as you revise:

• Will my writing be interesting to my reader? Can I make it more interesting?

• Do I care about my topic? How can I show this to my reader?

• Will my reader be able to "hear" my unique voice?

Before you finish revising your own paper, look over the writing below and on the following page. On this page, you can see examples of writing that might interest any reader. On the following page, you can read another writer's ideas about keeping the reader's interest.

The examples below show different ways that students using *The Multicultural Workshop* made their writing interesting to their readers—with vivid details, with analysis and opinion, with their unique voices:

❶

…I liked the sea very much, but it also scared me, especially when the thunder of the waves woke me up in the middle of the night. In the evening, when a cool, soft breeze blew in from the sea, it smelled like fresh shellfish. I used to contemplate the sunsets. The best sunsets were in summer in San Juan. Then the sea, land, and sky would become bright red fire….

—Maria Castro

❷

…I like this story because it teaches me about family love, and I can relate it to my personal life. Yet, sometimes, I take family love for granted.

—Tien Thuy Le

❸

When I was a little child, my mom always told me, "You must study." Well, I didn't understand what she said, but I still studied hard to make my mom happy….

—Nga Nguyen

Keeping Writing Interesting

"Ho hum. Just a bunch of mumbo jumbo.[1] This writing is so boring. I couldn't care less[2] what the writer is trying to say. Big yawn. My teacher said I had to finish reading this assignment by tomorrow, so I'd better push ahead. Ha! Like a snowplow through cement."

Avoid boring writing.

I have felt this way many times. I imagine everyone has. Too many writers forget that they are writing for someone, a real person, on the other end. I have to remind myself of this central fact every time I write.

Remember your readers.

Keeping sentences short can help. I have to make sure that I'm not just filling up space. I also have to care about what I'm writing. Readers aren't dumb. I know they can tell if I'm not interested in my topic. Why should they pay attention, if I don't even like what I'm writing?

Show your readers you care.

Showing readers my own true feelings can keep them interested. If I express myself and my opinions, other people are more likely to care. They might not agree with me. My writing might anger them. But if they hear a real voice in my written words, they will probably continue reading. They won't fall asleep.

Express yourself.

Simple language is usually best. Using big words doesn't necessarily make a person sound smart. Big words can make a person sound self-important, a terrible way to sound. I think I can speak more clearly with simple language. If there is a clear, concise way to express an idea, then use it. I tell myself this constantly.

Use clear language.

—*Amanda Buege*

---

1 **mumbo jumbo**   nonsense
2 **couldn't care less**   don't care at all

ABOUT THE AUTHOR
Amanda Buege is a graduate student at the University of New Orleans. There, she studies creative writing, literature, and composition theory. She also works with ESL students in the UNO Writing Lab.

UNIT THREE
Choices

In this unit you will read four selections related to the theme of choice.

- What are some of the choices people make at different times in their lives?
- Which are the hardest choices? Why?

CHAPTER ONE

Looking at the Bright Side

1. Class Work. Read the information below and answer the questions.

An optimist is a person who focuses on positive things. In a difficult situation, an optimist looks for the good things that might happen. Which of these people do you think is an optimist? Why?

The glass of water is half-full.

The glass of water is half-empty.

2. Pair Work. Look at the bright side of these situations. Think of something good that might result.

   Example: You've just lost your job.

   _____*Maybe I'll find a better job.*_____

   a. You wrecked your car last week.

   _____

   b. You and the person you hoped to marry have just broken up.

   _____

   c. You broke your right arm a few days ago.

   _____

   Read your ideas aloud to the class.

3. Pair Work. Read the title and the first paragraph of the folk tale on the next page. Why do you think the woman worries about her two sons? List several possibilities.

   _____

   _____

   _____

   _____

   _____

   _____

   _____

   _____

   Compare predictions with your classmates.

READING STRATEGY:
Predicting
See page 181.

4. Class Work. Read the folk tale to check your predictions.

Umbrellas and Straw Shoes

(A Korean Folk Tale)

There once was a woman who was constantly worrying about her two sons who were peddlers. The oldest sold umbrellas and the youngest, straw shoes.

One day after the long rainy season had ended, a neighbor stopped in to say hello. "Don't you feel great now that the rainy season is finally over," she greeted the woman.

"Well, I don't know. It just makes me worry."

"What do you mean it makes you worry?"

"Well, as you know, my oldest son sells umbrellas. So, with the weather like this, I'm afraid he won't be able to sell any."

On a rainy day a week or so later, the neighbor stopped in again. "After all those scorching hot days, isn't this rain nice? It has certainly cooled things down a lot," she said with a smile. "Don't you feel better now?"

"No, not at all," replied the woman glumly. "The rain just makes me worry."

"But why do you have to worry?" asked the neighbor.

"Because my second son sells straw shoes. Do you think anyone will buy straw shoes now that the ground is so muddy?"

The neighbor shook her head back and forth and smiled. "So, you worry when it rains, and you worry when it doesn't."

"Yes, that's right. I want both of my sons to do well. So how can I not worry?"

The two women were silent for a while. Then the neighbor slapped her knee. "I know how to solve your problem. You just do what I say and then you won't have to worry. Now listen. When it's cloudy or rainy, just say to yourself, 'Oh, how nice! My first son should be able to sell lots of umbrellas.' And, when it's nice and sunny, just say, 'Oh, how nice! My second son should be able to sell lots of straw shoes.' You see, you have always thought negatively, not positively. From now own you should look at the bright side of things. If you think that way, then you won't have to worry."

"Why that's true. I have always looked at the bad side of things. From now on I'm going to look at the bright side."

And in that way the woman learned the power of positive thinking and was forever happy.

❋ ✦ ❊ ✦ ❊ ✦ ❊ ✦ ❊

READING STRATEGY:
Using Context
See page 184.

5. **Pair Work.** Role-play the two characters in the story. One person reads the neighbor's lines and one person reads the mother's lines.

6. **On Your Own.** The sentences below are from the folk tale. Use context to guess the meaning of each **boldfaced** word. Then compare ideas with your classmates.

a. *There once was a woman who was constantly worrying about her two sons who were **peddlers**. The oldest sold umbrellas and the youngest, straw shoes.*

My guess: _____

_____

b. *"After all those scorching hot days, isn't this rain nice? It has certainly cooled things down a lot," she said with a smile. "Don't you feel better now?"*
   *"No, not at all," replied the woman **glumly**. "The rain just makes me worry."*

My guess: _____

_____

c. *"Do you think anyone will buy straw shoes now that the ground is so **muddy**?"*

My guess: _____

_____

d. *The two women were silent for a while. Then the neighbor **slapped** her knee. "I know how to solve your problem."*

My guess: _____

_____

7. Pair Work.

a. Much of the story "Umbrellas and Straw Shoes" is dialogue. In a dialogue, writers use quotation marks before and after a person's words.

Example:

> "The rain has certainly cooled things down a lot," the neighbor said with a smile. "Don't you feel better now?"
>
> "No, not at all," replied the woman glumly. "The rain just makes me worry."

Without looking back at the story, add quotation marks to the dialogue below.

But why do you have to worry? asked the neighbor.

Because my second son sells straw shoes, answered the woman. Do you think anyone will buy shoes now that the ground is so muddy?

The neighbor shook her head back and forth and smiled. So, you worry when it rains, and you worry when it doesn't.

Yes, that's right, the woman replied. I want both of my sons to do well. So how can I not worry?

Ask your teacher for feedback.

b. Sometimes the writer gives information to help you know how a character feels. Choose a word to complete each of the sentences below. More than one answer is possible.

glumly   with a smile   excitedly

happily   with a frown

• "I found $50.00," she said _____

• "I just lost my job," he said _____

• "I passed the test," he said _____

• "I don't have any money," she replied _____

• "We're going to get married," she announced _____

_____

Read your sentences to the class.

✳✦✳✦✳✦✳✦

CRITICAL THINKING
STRATEGY:
*Applying What
You Know*
See page 186.

CRITICAL THINKING
STRATEGY:
Analyzing
See page 185.

8. **Pair Work.** On another piece of paper, add to the folk tale. Tell what the two women say on the next rainy day. Use quotation marks before and after each person's words. Then exchange writing with another pair.

Example:

On a rainy day a week later, the neighbor stopped in again….

9. **Journal Writing.** Write about a time when you were worried about something. Here are some questions you might think about:

• What were you worried about?

• What did you do?

• How did you feel?

• Did you think negatively or positively?

10. **Writing Assignment.** Write a dialogue between an optimist and a pessimist. Here are some suggestions to help you get started:

┌─────────────────────────┐
│ ❋ ✦ ❋ ✦ ❋ ✦ ❋ ✦ ❋   │
├─────────────────────────┤
│ **WRITING STRATEGY:**   │
│ *Developing a*   │
│ *Point of View*   │
│ See page 170.   │
└─────────────────────────┘

a. Class Work. Think of different ways to complete this sentence. List your ideas on the board.

My friend is constantly worrying because _____

_____

b. Pair Work. Choose one of the problems from the list on the board. Role-play two friends discussing this problem. One person looks at the negative side of things. One person looks at the bright side of things.

Example:

> *Person A: What's the matter? You look worried.*
>
> *Person B: I am. I don't have any money.*
>
> *Person A: Why don't you get a job?*
>
> *Person B: I'd like to get a job but no one will hire me.*
>
> *Person A: …*

c. On Your Own. Write a dialogue between the two people. Use quotation marks around each person's words. Give information about how each person feels.

d. On Your Own. Add an introduction to the dialogue. Describe the problem.

Example:

> *There was once a young woman who was constantly worrying because she didn't have any money. As soon as she got some money, she spent it. One day she met a friend on the street.*
> *"What's the matter?" her friend asked. "You look worried."*
> *"I am," she answered glumly. "I don't have any money."*
> *"Why don't you get a job?" her friend suggested.*
> *"Impossible," said the young woman unhappily. "No one will ever hire me."*

e. Read Around. Get together with a group of classmates. Take turns reading each other's writing.

f. Place your writing in your writing folder.

C H A P T E R   T W O

Choosing Goals

CRITICAL THINKING STRATEGY:
Classifying
See page 187.

1. Class Work. Read the information below.

A *goal* is something you want to obtain or accomplish.

A *short-term goal* is something you want in the near future.

A *long-term goal* is something you want in the distant future.

Put these goals into the two groups below.

I want to become a doctor.

I plan to return to my country next year.

I want to find a new apartment.

I plan to have my own business.

I hope to find a job soon.

I hope to have a large family.

I hope to earn a Ph.D.

I hope to do well in my classes this semester.

Short-Term Goals	Long-Term Goals
to find a new apartment	

2. On Your Own. List your own short-term and long-term goals. Then tell a partner about them.

Short-Term Goals	**Long-Term Goals**
_____	_____
_____	_____
_____	_____
_____	_____

3. Group Work. Read the title of the newspaper article on page 82 and answer the questions below. Then share your ideas with the class.

a. From the title, what do you know about "this graduate"?

b. What do you think this article is about?

4. On Your Own. Read the newspaper article on the following page to check your predictions.

READING STRATEGY:
Predicting
See page 180.

At 81, This Graduate Proves It's Always Possible to Learn More

by Gary Libman

Los Angeles Times

LOS ANGELES – Jesus Ibarra was confused by the elderly man in the skullcap.[1]

He was obviously much older than other students at Central Adult High School. And he was an Anglo[2] on a campus where most students are Latinos, blacks, and Asian-Americans.

"I asked myself what he was doing here," says Ibarra, 21, of Los Angeles. "I thought he was a volunteer.[3] The first time I talked to him, I asked a question in English, and he answered in Spanish. I thought he was white and Jewish. I never imagined that he would speak Spanish."

Jacob Blitzstein surprised his fellow students all the time. He isn't some stuffy guy, despite his trim gray beard and conservative clothes.

Blitzstein is warm and gregarious. He likes to hear a good joke—and loves to tell a good story. He is tough, especially when it comes to pursuing his dream.

Recently, that dream came true. At a ceremony attended by two of his children and three grandchildren, Blitzstein, 81, graduated from high school.

After Principal Lanny Nelms handed him the diploma and announced his age, Blitzstein waved to the audience and cried.

And why not? He's probably the oldest Central High graduate since the school opened in 1974. Although no records of such things are kept, a Los Angeles district spokesman says Blitzstein is the oldest graduate he's ever heard of.

Earning his diploma took 10 years, during which the retired store owner suffered a stroke[4] and two bouts of pneumonia,[5] had two pacemakers[6] installed, and lost his wife and two siblings.

He kept to his task for a reason. School "is the best medicine you can have," he says. "You have something on your mind—a goal."…

With his diploma in hand, Blitzstein maintains that he's not through yet.

"You know something? I'm going to college," he told a visitor recently. He has checked out West Los Angeles and Santa Monica community colleges and says he hopes to transfer from there to a four-year school.

"It's not a joke," he says. "If I live to the year 2000, maybe I'll be a doctor."

---

1 **skullcap**   a hat worn by some people of the Jewish religion

2 **Anglo**   a white American who is not of Hispanic descent

3 **volunteer**   a person who works for no payment

4 **stroke**   a sudden blockage of blood (and therefore oxygen) to the brain, which can cause loss of movement in parts of the body

5 **pneumonia**   a serious disease of the lungs

6 **pacemaker**   a small mechanical device that regulates heartbeats

5. Pair Work. Scan the article on page 82 to find the information below. Then compare ideas with another pair. Show where in the article you found the information.

READING STRATEGY:
Scanning
See page 182.

Jacob Blitzstein

Age _____

Profession _____

Religion _____

Marital Status _____

Languages _____

Personality _____

_____

Health _____

_____

Goals _____

_____

6. On Your Own. Read these sentences from the article and the dictionary definitions. Use context to choose the correct meaning of each **boldfaced** word.

READING STRATEGY:
Using Context
See page 184.

a. *He isn't some* **stuffy** *guy, despite his trim gray beard and conservative clothes.*

In this sentence *stuffy* means _____

stuffy / *adj* -ier, -iest ❶ having air which is not fresh: a *stuffy* room ❷ (of ideas) dull, old-fashioned, etc.

b. *He is **tough**, especially when it comes to pursuing his dream.*

In this sentence, *tough* means _____

tough / adj ❶ strong; not easily weakened: *Only tough breeds of sheep can live in the mountains.* ❷ difficult to cut or eat: *tough meat* ❸ difficult to do; demanding effort: *a tough lesson/job* ❹ rough; hard: *The government will get tough with people who avoid paying taxes.* ❺ *informal* too bad; unfortunate: *Tough luck!*

c. *Earning his diploma took 10 years, during which the retired store owner suffered a stroke and two **bouts** of pneumonia….*

In this sentence, *bouts* means _____

bout / n ❶ a short period of fierce activity or illness: *a bout of drinking (=drinking alcohol)/several bouts of fever* ❷ a boxing match

d. *With his diploma in hand, Blitzstein **maintains** that he's not **through** yet.*

In this sentence, *maintains* means _____

In this sentence, *through* means _____

maintain / v ❶ to continue to have, do, etc., as before: *He maintained his interest in football all his life.* ❷ to support with money: *to maintain a family* ❸ to keep in good condition; take care of: *the high cost of maintaining an old house* ❹ [+ (that) / to be] to (continue to) argue for (an opinion): *Some people still maintain that the earth is flat.*

through / adv ❶ in at one side and out at the other: *I opened the gate and let them through.* ❷ all the way from beginning to end: *She read the letter through.* ❸ to a successful end: *I failed the examination, but she got through.* (=passed) ❹ connected by telephone: *"Can you put me through to Mr. Jones?"* ❺ [with] to or at the end; finished: *Are you through with your work yet?*

— definitions adapted from
Longman Dictionary of American English

Get feedback from your teacher and classmates.

7. **Journal Writing.** What's your reaction to the article on page 82? Write about it in your journal. Here are some questions you might think about:

   • What interested you most in this article?

   • Would you like to know Jacob Blitzstein? Why or why not?

   • Why do you think this article appeared in the newspaper? Is it newsworthy?

   • When you are 81, what goals do you think you will have?

   Get together with your classmates and share ideas from your quick-writing.

CRITICAL THINKING STRATEGY: *Evaluating* See page 189.

8. **Class Work.** A summary is a short version of a story in your own words. It gives only the most important information. It does not include unnecessary details. Which of these ideas would you include in a summary of the article on page 82?

   ❏ 1. Jacob Blitzstein wears a skullcap.

   ❏ 2. He's an Anglo who speaks Spanish.

   ❏ 3. He wears conservative clothes.

   ❏ 4. He is 81 years old.

   ❏ 5. He has just graduated from high school.

   ❏ 6. His children and grandchildren came to the graduation ceremony.

   ❏ 7. He got his diploma from Principal Lanny Nelms.

   ❏ 8. He cried when he got his diploma.

   ❏ 9. He is probably the oldest person to graduate from Central High School.

   ❏ 10. It took him ten years to earn his high-school diploma.

   ❏ 11. He didn't stop studying even though he got sick several times and his wife died.

   ❏ 12. He had pneumonia twice while he was studying for his diploma.

READING STRATEGY: *Summarizing* See page 183.

❏ 13. He thinks that having a goal keeps you healthy.

❏ 14. He has future plans—to go to college and to become a doctor.

❏ 15. He is thinking about going to West Los Angeles Community College.

9. **On Your Own.** Use the most important ideas above to write a summary of the article for a friend outside of class. Use your own words.

10. **Writing Assignment.**

WRITING STRATEGY:
Developing a
Point of View
See page 170.

a. Class Work. Writers have a point of view—attitudes and judgments about the topic. What do you think Gary Libman's (the writer of the newspaper article) point of view is? How do you know?

b. On Your Own. One way to explore a topic or an event is to look at it from different points of view. Choose one of the people below. Describe the graduation ceremony at Central High School from this person's point of view. Your description should reveal something about the speaker's personality, attitudes, and judgments. Write your description in the first person.

   • Jacob Blitzstein

   • Jesus Ibarra

   • Lanny Nelms

   • Jacob Blitzstein's grandchild

c. Read your description to a classmate. See if your classmate can guess who the speaker is.

d. Place your writing in your writing folder.

CHAPTER THREE

Choosing a Mate

1. **Class Work.** In American English, your *mate* is your marriage partner. What do you think are the characteristics of a good mate? List
your ideas on the board.

❊ ★ ❊ ★ ❊ ★ ❊ ★ ❊

WRITING STRATEGY:
Listing Ideas
See page 172.

A Good Mate

is a good listener

_____

_____

_____

2. **Group Work.** Get together with several classmates of the same
gender. List the characteristics of a good mate in order from the
most important to the least important.

❊ ★ ❊ ★ ❊ ★ ❊ ★ ❊

**CRITICAL THINKING
STRATEGY:**
Evaluating
See page 189.

Most important: _____

_____

_____

_____

_____

_____

_____

_____

Least important: _____

Compare lists with the other groups in your class.

3. Group Work. Read the sentence below. What do you think the person will say? List several ideas. Then read them to the class.

"If you want to marry me," my fiancé(e) said, "Here's what you'll

have to do: _____

_____

_____

_____

_____

_____"

4. Class Work. Listen as your teacher reads the following poem. Then read it aloud to a partner.

My Rules

If you want to marry me, here's what you'll have to do
You must learn how to make a perfect chicken dumpling stew
And you must sew my holey socks and you must soothe my
troubled mind
And develop the knack for scratching my back
And keep my shoes spotlessly shined
And while I rest you must rake up the leaves
And when it is hailing and snowing
You must shovel the walk, and be still when I talk
And—hey, where are you going??

—Shel Silverstein

5. Class Work. Identify the activities in the photographs below. Then, take turns pantomiming the tasks as the poem is read. Let your classmates guess the task.

6. Class Work. What's your reaction to the poem? Share ideas with your classmates. Here are some questions you can talk about:

- Do you think the speaker of the poem is a man or a woman? Why?

- Would you advise someone to marry this person? Why or why not?

- This poem is often included in poetry books for children. What message might this poem have for young people?

CRITICAL THINKING STRATEGY: *Interpreting* See page 190.

7. Group Work.

a. Brainstorm a list of rules for choosing a mate. Your rules can be serious or silly. Choose one person in your group to record your ideas.

b. Choose ideas from your list to write a poem. Read your poem aloud to each other and make changes until you like the way the poem sounds.

c. Choose one person in your group to read your poem aloud to the class.

8. Class Work. The title of the poem on the next page is "Winner." Give examples of a "winner."

Examples: *someone who comes in first in a race*
someone who applies for a job and gets it

9. Class Work. Read the following poem aloud several times.

Winner

Mrs. Macey worked behind
the meat counter at Janelli's Market
until her husband took up
with the Methodist[1] organist,
leaving her to wear embarrassment
like split pants.
Then she won the Am Vets'[2] raffle—
a trip to Miami
during the Fourth of July[3] weekend—
and never returned.

Instead
she sent a postcard of flamingos
on the lawn of an awninged hotel
that Mr. Janelli butcher-taped
on the meat case:
"Met a wonderful man
wears a slender moustache,
plays trumpet in a jazz band,
and calls me Cara Mia.[4]"

— *Paul B. Janeczko*

---

1 **Methodist**   a member of a Protestant Christian religious group
2 **AmVet**   an organization of American veterans, or people who fought in wars
3 **Fourth of July**   a U.S. holiday that celebrates the country's independence from Great Britain
4 **Cara Mia**   "My dear" in Italian

10. **Pair Work.** What do you know about the people below? List information from the poem.

READING STRATEGY:
*Taking Notes
in a Chart*
See page 183.

Mr. Macey	Mrs. Macey	Mr. Janelli	The Jazz Player
	worked in a grocery store		

Compare charts with your classmates.

11. **Group Work.** What's your reaction to the poem? Here are some questions to think about:

- Who is the winner in the poem? Why do you think this?

- What did Mr. Janelli do with the postcard? Why?

- What choices did the people in the poem make? Which ones do you think were good choices? Bad choices?

Report your group's answers to the class.

CRITICAL THINKING
STRATEGY:
Interpreting
See page 190.

12. Writing Assignment.

a. Class Work. The poem "Winner" is a summary of a complex series of events. It gives the most important information, but it doesn't give many details. What other information would you like to find out about the people in the story? List your questions on the board.

   Example: *How did Mrs. Macey feel when her husband left her?*

b. Class Work. Suggest answers to your questions.

c. Journal Writing. Imagine that you are Mrs. Macey. Quickwrite for five minutes. Explain what happened to you. Tell how you feel about these events.

d. In writing, tell the story from Mrs. Macey's point of view. Use ideas from your quickwriting.

e. Read Around. Get together with a group of classmates. Take turns reading each other's writing.

f. Place your writing in your writing folder.

CHAPTER FOUR

Influencing Your Choices

1. **Class Work.** Think about your day yesterday. What choices did you make during the day? List your ideas on the board.

   Examples: *when to get up in the morning*
   what to wear

   Think about one of the choices you made yesterday. What influenced your decision? Tell your classmates.

2. **Journal Writing.** Write about the advertisement below. Here are some questions you might think about:

   - What's your reaction to the picture?

   - How does the picture make you feel? Why?

   - What is this advertisement trying to influence you to do?

   Read one idea from your journal writing to your classmates.

   > **CRITICAL THINKING STRATEGY:**
   > *Analyzing*
   > See page 185.

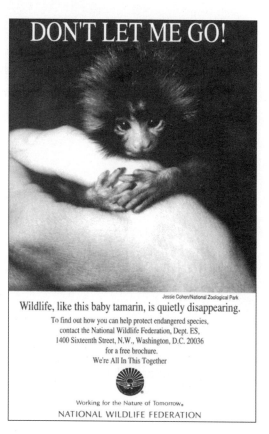

DON'T LET ME GO!

Jessie Cohen/National Zoological Park

Wildlife, like this baby tamarin, is quietly disappearing.
To find out how you can help protect endangered species,
contact the National Wildlife Federation, Dept. ES,
1400 Sixteenth Street, N.W., Washington, D.C. 20036
for a free brochure.
We're All In This Together

Working for the Nature of Tomorrow.
NATIONAL WILDLIFE FEDERATION

3. **Group Work.** Look again at the advertisement on page 95 and answer these questions:

a. What could you say to influence your teacher to send money to the address in the ad?

It will make you feel good to send money.

_____

_____

_____

_____

_____

_____

Read your group's ideas to the class.

b. Advertisements influence people by appealing to their emotions, or feelings. How does the advertisement on page 95 make you feel?

❏ nostalgic   ❏ proud

❏ sad   ❏ ashamed

❏ guilty   ❏ envious

Compare ideas with your classmates.

4. **Group Work.** Do you agree with the statements below? Why or why not?

• Cosmetic advertisements are not selling skin cream; they are selling hope.

• Car advertisements are not selling automobiles; they are selling prestige.

Compare ideas with your classmates.

5. Group Work. Study the advertisement below. What do you think this advertisement is selling? Report your group's answer to the class.

CRITICAL THINKING
STRATEGY:
Analyzing
See page 185.

6. Class Work. Read the title and the first sentence of each paragraph on the next pages. Tell what you think the reading is about.

7. On Your Own. Read pages 98–99 to check your prediction.

READING STRATEGY:
Previewing
See page 181.

from An Appeal to the Emotions

by Ann E. Weiss

Advertisers know that their most effective selling tool is a successful appeal to people's emotions. According to one writer, an ad can appeal to the emotions on any of three distinct levels. On the first level are emotions that people admire: patriotism, nostalgia, kindness toward mothers, children, dogs, and so on. On the second level are emotions of which people aren't so proud: inadequacy, guilt, shame, anxiety, alarm, fear. On the third are emotions that few like to admit to: self-interest, ambition, envy, pride, vanity, greed, self-preservation.

Flip through almost any national magazine and you'll find ads that appeal to each of these emotional levels. At the beginning of the magazine, an ad for a hotel chain[1] depicts a peaceful moonlit countryside. From the window of a farmhouse, light streams out into the night. "They left a light in the window…It's the light that will lead you home." Pure nostalgia.

Turn a few pages. Gazing out pathetically[2] is a child—"doomed to poverty"—unless people send money to the charity[3] that paid for the ad. Only someone with a heart of stone could fail to be touched by pity for this child. That's a level one appeal. At the same time, we begin to think of our own affluent[4] lifestyles. Most of us can only guess at the desperation of this child's life. Why do we have so much—and she so little? We're ashamed of our ease and comfort, and we feel guilty. That's a level two appeal.

A few pages farther on is a two-page ad for an expensive blend of whiskey. "Long after you've forgotten the few extra dollars," proclaims the headline, someone will remember that

---

1 **hotel chain**   a group of hotels under one ownership
2 **pathetically**   causing a feeling of sadness, pity, or sorrow
3 **charity**   an organization that gives help to the poor
4 **affluent**   wealthy

you gave him this whiskey. This is one gift that will make a big impression. Anyone who receives it from you will know that you have good taste—and money to spare.[5] A level three appeal to vanity.

Copywriters[6] don't hesitate to push products by playing on people's secret fears and wishes. As one pointed out, "The cosmetic manufacturers are not selling lanolin,[7] they are selling hope…. We no longer buy oranges, we buy vitality.[8] We do not just buy an auto, we buy prestige.[9]"

This selection is taken from the book The School on Madison Avenue.

---

5 **money to spare**   more money than you need
6 **copywriters**   people who write advertisements
7 **lanolin**   a fatty substance used in soaps and cosmetics
8 **vitality**   energy
9 **prestige**   the power to command admiration from others

Three Levels of Emotions

Level 3

Emotions that few people like to admit to:
self-interest
envy
vanity
ambition
pride
greed
self-preservation

Level 2

Emotions of which people aren't so proud:
inadequacy
shame
alarm
guilt
anxiety
fear

Level 1

Emotions that people admire:
patriotism
kindness
nostalgia

⸎ ★ ⸎ ★ ⸎ ★ ⸎ ★ ⸎

READING STRATEGY:
Finding Main Ideas
See page 178.

8. Class Work. Read the information below and answer the questions.

The topic or subject of the reading on pages 98–99 is *advertising*. The author of this reading has information and ideas about advertising to share with her readers. The most important idea that the author wants to communicate about the topic is called the main idea.

What is the main idea of this reading? Is the main idea stated in the reading? If so, where?

9. On Your Own. How does the writer organize her ideas? Reread pages 98–99 and take notes in this chart.

Paragraph	Topic (What is the paragraph about?)
1	*three levels of emotions that ads appeal to*
2	
3	
4	
5	

Compare charts with your classmates.

10. Pair Work. Match the comments below with an emotion from the list.

Emotions

ambition	greed	inadequacy	self-interest
envy	guilt	nostalgia	vanity

_____envy_____   a. "I wish I looked like her."

_____   b. "I grew up in a wonderful small town in New Mexico. It was a perfect place for children."

_____   c. "I have beautiful hair."

_____   d. "My brother has a serious medical problem. Why am I so healthy when my brother isn't?"

_____   e. "I'll do anything to get that job."

_____   f. "I'm rich but not rich enough."

_____   g. "There is nothing I can do to help you."

_____   h. "If my friend moves to New York, I will have a free place to stay when I go there on business."

Compare ideas with your classmates.

11. Journal Writing. Choose a magazine advertisement that interests you. Bring it to class. In writing, describe the picture to your classmates.

Example:

This advertisement shows a handsome man standing with a beautiful woman. The man is wearing a suit and the woman is wearing a beautiful dress. The man is holding the woman close to him and it looks as if they are in love. They both look very happy.

Read your description to the class. See if your classmates can guess what the advertisement is trying to sell.

12. **Writing Assignment.** How do advertisers try to influence people? Explore this question by studying several magazine advertisements. Then write your ideas for your classmates to read. You can follow the steps below for more specific writing suggestions.

   a. Choose one type of product, for example, cars, perfume, or sports clothes. Study different advertisements for this product. Take notes on your reaction to each advertisement.

   b. Add information about each advertisement to a chart like this:

Advertisement	What message does it try to communicate to the reader?	How does it communicate the message?
Joy Perfume	You will have interesting experiences if you wear this perfume.	A woman is floating on a rope ladder in the sky.

c. In writing, explain how you think advertisers try to influence people. Use ideas and examples from your notes and chart.

d. Exchange papers with a classmate. Read your partner's paper.

e. Attach the advertisements to your writing. Place your writing in your writing folder.

UNIT THREE
Final Project

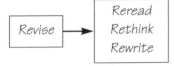

For your final project, choose one of your first drafts from Unit 3 to revise. Here are some questions you might think about as you revise your writing:

- What do you like about your first draft? What are its strengths?

- Does it give your reader enough information?

- Is it clear?

- Will it be interesting to your reader?

As you revise your paper, pay special attention to your introductory paragraph. Remember that your introduction is the place where you get your reader's attention. Try experimenting with different ways of writing your introduction:

- Start with a question that gets your reader's attention.

- Try giving the most important information first. Hit your reader with the facts or the main idea. (See "An Appeal to the Emotions," pages 98–99.)

- Tell an anecdote. (See "Without Hesitation," pages 26–27.)

- Start with a sentence that makes your reader ask "Why?" (See "At 81, This Graduate Proves It's Always Possible to Learn More," page 82.)

For more ideas on writing introductions, look over the next three pages. On page 105, you can look at some different ways that students using *The Multicultural Workshop* wrote their introductions. On pages 106–107, you can read one writer's thoughts on writing introductions.

These examples show different ways that students using *The Multicultural Workshop* began their essays:

> When I looked at myself in the mirror this morning, I realized that today I have more wrinkles around my eyes, mouth, and neck than I had ten years ago.

(first sentence in an essay on aging by Maria A. Castro)

> When I was a child, I had many dreams. Being a teacher when I grew up was one of my favorites because I live in a family of teachers.

(first sentences in an essay about the writer's plans for the future by Tien Thuy Le)

> Once, four years ago, I found myself in a difficult situation. I wasn't able to buy books for my studies because I didn't have any money. I was very worried. The books were expensive and I had lost my job. I felt glum and anxious. I didn't know what to do.

(introduction to an essay about positive and negative thinking by Diana Echenique Janowsky)

> Life is like waves on the ocean and people are like ships. Sometimes the water is calm and sometimes it is uncertain.

(first sentences in an essay about events in the writer's life by Hoang Dang)

Before you start revising your paper, read one writer's ideas about writing introductions on the next page.

Writing Introductions

Be creative.

Developing an introduction is usually fun, but not always easy. Introductions are perfect places to be really creative. What I try to keep in mind is my audience. I want to grab my readers and get their attention. Sometimes being quiet works best, almost as if whispering a secret to my audience. Other times I like to yell a little to make sure my readers are awake. Yet other times I'll tell them "straight out.[1]" I'll say, "Here it is, the truth. I won't lead you in circles."

Make choices.

All these options[2] make introductions enjoyable—and hard. I want to make sure I choose an interesting way to begin. I want my audience to care about what I am saying. I also think of what the word "introduction" means. My subject shouldn't just appear on the page, out of the blue.[3] Just plopping my subject on the paper would be the same as bringing a stranger to a party and not telling anyone the stranger's name. I try to remember to be a good host when it comes to introductions.

Paint a picture.

I often begin with a description. When I can't think of any other way to start an essay, I know that I can always create a picture in my reader's mind. I can set the mood: *The wind outside is blowing, and tree branches are scraping against my windows. It's raining. The electricity has gone out, and I'm trying to cook dinner by candle-*

---

1 **straight out**   directly
2 **options**   choices
3 **out of the blue**   with no introduction

light. Or I can put my reader in an exact place: *a little outdoor cafe in New Orleans. The waiters wear starched white shirts and the smell of seafood drifts out from the kitchen. My friend and I sit near a large palm tree. We're having a late lunch of Caesar salads and crusty French bread.*

Either one of these descriptions might lead into an essay about food and nutrition, or perhaps an essay about eating at home versus eating out. What about that yelling introduction I talked about? I could write: *Did you know that three out of every four Americans don't get enough vitamins?* Or the whisper introduction: *That delicious piece of chocolate cake is calling you from behind the refrigerator door....*

Lead into your essay.

Introductions allow me to be versatile, and I like that. If a writer can make an introduction interesting, half the writing battle is over. The reader is hooked.

Hook your reader.

—*Amanda Buege*

ABOUT THE AUTHOR
Amanda Buege is a graduate student at the University of New Orleans. There, she studies creative writing, literature, and composition theory. She also works with ESL students in the UNO Writing Lab. She wrote down her thoughts on writing for students using *The Multicultural Workshop.*

UNIT FOUR
Relationships

In this unit you will read four selections related to the theme of relationships.

- Study the people in each picture. What do you think their relationship is? Why?

CHAPTER ONE

Family Responsibilities

❋ ★ ❋ ★ ❋ ★ ❋ ★ ❋

WRITING STRATEGY:
*Taking Notes
in a Chart*
See page 177.

1. **Class Work.** What do the people in a family do for each other? What are their responsibilities? For example, what does a wife do for her husband? Write your ideas in the chart below:

Family Responsibilities

	Mother/Wife	Father/Husband	Children/Siblings
What does a mother/wife do for...?	✕	*takes care of when sick*	*feeds, clothes*
What does a father/husband do for...?		✕	
What do children/siblings do for...?			

2. Journal Writing. Choose someone in your family. List several things this person has done for you. Then quickwrite about the ideas on your list.

WRITING STRATEGY:
Quickwriting
See page 176.

Example: *Things my mother did*
planned great birthday parties
made clothes for us
took us camping

When I was a child, my mother planned wonderful birthday parties for us. Not ordinary birthday parties. They were special events. One year she planned a treasure hunt for my birthday….

Choose something from your quickwriting to read or tell a classmate about.

3. Group Work. Work together to come up with a solution to this problem from the folk tale on pages 112–113:

READING STRATEGY:
Predicting
See page 181.

A man wants to help his brother. His brother has just gotten married and he has a lot of expenses. The man wants to give his brother a sack of rice, but he knows his brother will not accept it. What do you think the man should do?

Choose one person to report your group's answer to the class.

4. On Your Own. Read the folk tale to find out how one man helps his brother.

Two Brothers

(A Korean Folk Tale)

In times gone by there lived two brothers who were very fond of[1] each other. Their father had died years before and together they took care of their widowed mother. When she died, the two brothers divided everything evenly.

Together the two brothers worked diligently in their fields from sunup to sundown. Every autumn they had the largest harvest[2] in the valley.

One autumn evening, after they had sacked and divided the rice harvest, the older brother thought, "Brother has lots of expenses since he just got married a few months ago. I think I will put a sack of rice in his storehouse and not tell him. If I offered it to him, I'm sure he would never accept it." So, late that night, he put a sack of rice on his A-frame carrier and took it to his brother's storehouse.

The next day, while tidying up his own storehouse, the older brother discovered that he had the same number of sacks of rice as the day before. "That's odd," he said, shaking his head,

---

1 **fond of**   caring about
2 **harvest**   the amount of food gathered from the fields

"I'm sure I took a sack of rice to Brother's house last night." He counted his sacks again. "Well," he said, scratching the back of his head, "I'll just take him another one tonight."

So, late that night, he carried a sack of rice to his brother's house.

The next morning, he was again surprised to find he had the same number of sacks as before. He shook his head over and over and decided he would take his brother another sack that night.

After a late dinner he put the rice on his A-frame and set out for his brother's house. It was a full moon and he could see the path quite clearly. Ahead he saw a man carrying something bulky.[3]

"Why, Brother!" they both called out at the same time. The two brothers put down their sacks and laughed long and hard. They both understood the mystery behind their unchanging number of sacks of rice. The younger brother thought his older brother needed the rice because he had a larger family.

---

3 **bulky** large and difficult to carry

READING STRATEGY:
Making a Story Outline
See page 179.

5. **On Your Own.** Make a story outline in the diagram below. Then compare outlines with your classmates.

Title: ***Two Brothers***

MAIN CHARACTERS
Who are the people in the story?

SETTING (Place and Time)
Where are they?
When does the story take place?

PROBLEM
What is the problem in the story?

PLOT (Action)

What happened in the beginning of the story?	*What happened in the middle of the story?*	*What happened at the end?*

6. **Pair Work**. Look back at the folk tale to find the words below. Use context to guess the meaning of each word. Then look up each word in a dictionary.

READING STRATEGY:
Using Context
See page 184.

a. Paragraph 1: widowed

My guess: _____

Dictionary definition: _____

b. Paragraph 2: diligently

My guess: _____

Dictionary definition: _____

c. Paragraph 4: tidying up

My guess: _____

Dictionary definition: _____

d. Paragraph 4: odd

My guess: _____

Dictionary definition: _____

e. Paragraph 7: set out for

My guess: _____

Dictionary definition: _____

Compare ideas with your classmates.

7. **Journal Writing.** What does this folk tale say to you about family relationships? What lesson do you think it tries to teach? Explore your ideas as you write in your journal. When you have finished writing, look over your writing and choose one idea to read to the class.

CRITICAL THINKING STRATEGY:
Synthesizing
See page 191.

8. **Writing Assignment.** A narrative is a piece of writing that tells a story. Follow these steps to write your own narrative.

   a. Think of times when people in your family helped you in some way. List them.

   b. Choose one event from your list.

   c. Describe this event in a story outline (see Activity 5).

   d. Use your outline to tell your story to a partner.

   e. Write the story for your classmates to read.

   f. Read Around. Get together with a group of classmates. Take turns reading each other's story.

   g. Place your writing in your writing folder.

CHAPTER TWO

Family Customs

1. **Pair Work.**

   a. Think of a custom in your family—something your family does or did habitually, every day, every year, etc.

   b. Tell your partner about this family custom.

   c. Get together with another pair. Tell them about your partner's family custom.

   Example:

   > *On Sundays in my family, my father always cooked breakfast. No one could go into the kitchen while he was cooking. That was his rule. He always made a big mess in the kitchen, so no one wanted to go into the kitchen anyway. But breakfast was always delicious.*

2. **Pair Work.** The stories on the next two pages tell about family customs. Read only the titles of the stories. Choose one title and answer the questions below. Then share your ideas with the class.

   • What do you think the story is about?

   • Does the title make you think of a custom in your family? Tell your partner about it.

   > **READING STRATEGY:**
   > *Previewing*
   > See page 181.

3. **Journal Writing.** Read the stories on pages 118–119 and take notes in a chart like this.

   > **READING STRATEGY:**
   > *Reading for Specific Information*
   > See page 182.

Title	Custom	Frequency	Your Reaction
The Brittany Lighthouse	*grandfather bakes a special cake; he holds up the cake and the kids walk around him*	*every summer*	*interesting; there's nothing like this in my family; where did the grandfather get the idea to do this?*

Family Customs

The Brittany Lighthouse

My grandparents live in Brittany, a region situated on the Atlantic Ocean in the northwestern part of France. They live in a seaside village by a little port with a lighthouse. People in the village like to walk around the lighthouse.

People in Brittany bake a special cake called "le phare breton" (the Brittany lighthouse). Since I was a little girl, my grandfather has baked that cake every summer when my brother, my cousins, and I go to visit him. Whenever he bakes the cake, he says to all his grandchildren, "Let's walk around the lighthouse." We then stand up and walk around my grandfather while he holds the cake above his head.

Nowadays, even though all of his grandchildren are over 20, my grandfather still bakes his famous cake and we all stand up, walk around him, and laugh.

—Elsa Levenes

A Greek Wedding

In Greece, a wedding is a big event, especially in the islands. After the wedding mass, people gather outside the church to celebrate. Then they proceed to a nearby restaurant to continue the celebration. Marriages in my family and in other families have been like this for centuries.

During the celebration, the bride and groom stand on a table and dance traditional Greek dances. Others soon join them in dancing. While the newlyweds are dancing, people stick paper money in their clothes. They might end up with as much as $10,000, if they can dance for a very long time!

—Demetris Sevastopoulas

The Family Tree

For the past three years, members of my extended family—over a hundred of them—have gathered every Tuesday evening for a family "meeting." They meet to discuss the history of the family. Of course the real purpose is to get to know each other and to meet "new" relatives who have migrated into the area to farm neighboring land.

As a result of the Tuesday evening gathering, the family now gets together on holidays, for funerals, and at weddings. I hope this practice of meeting every week gets handed down in my family as a tradition.

—Yousif Khalid

"Las Mañanitas"

When my family moved to the United States, I had to stay home with one of my aunts. This aunt is a very sweet lady. As a matter of fact, I can say that I love Aunt Marieta as much as I love my mother. I lived with her for about three years before I came to the States.

During that time, we practiced a nice custom. Whenever anyone in Aunt Marieta's house had a birthday, we would sing "Las Mañanitas," a Spanish birthday song. Everyone in the family had to awaken the "birthday" person with "Las Mañanitas."

We had a little problem with my aunt's birthday though. My aunt's birth certificate said she was born on August 12, but my grandmother said that Aunt Marieta was born on August 11. My aunt claimed August 12 as her birthday because that's what the birth certificate said, but my grandmother insisted that she knew better than the birth certificate! So we decided to sing "Las Mañanitas" on both days. My poor aunt had to wake up to the same song two days in a row!

Now that I'm living in the States, we celebrate birthdays differently. But I always call Aunt Marieta on her birthday and she calls me on mine. We sing "Las Mañanitas" to each other over the telephone!

—*Claudia Zavala*

New Year's Eve

Years ago in Vietnam, my family would gather for dinner on New Year's Eve. My grandfather would always begin the conversation in the same way. He would remind all of his grandchildren not to quarrel and not to break any dishes during the first three days of the new year. He thought quarreling and breaking dishes during the first three days brought bad luck the whole year. Grandfather also told us that we were all one year older and more mature, so we had to be responsible for our actions.

My sister, brother, and I left Vietnam seventeen years ago, and my grandfather died eight years ago. We still try to follow his tradition of eating together on New Year's Eve, and we will pass this tradition on to our children and grandchildren.

—*S. Van Huynh*

Grandfather's Wine

When autumn comes to France, all the family meets for a weekend at my grandparents' farm in the Rhone Valley. During these two days, everyone goes into the vineyards to pick grapes. Early on a Saturday morning, each of us takes a knife and a basket. The tractor follows us pulling a wagon and we "feed" the wagon with our full baskets of grapes. Around 5 o'clock, we return to the farmhouse. The women go to the kitchen to prepare dinner. The men go to the barn to press the grapes and put the juice in big vats to ferment. The men select bottles of wine from last year's crop and carry them to the house to drink with dinner.

The wine my grandfather makes is very bad, but it is a passion for him. Everybody does his best to help my grandfather and nobody says how bad the wine really is. When dinner is ready, we all sit around the table. Even if we are tired, we eat, drink my grandfather's wine, talk, and sing until late into the night.

—*Lionel Biennier*

119

READING STRATEGY:
Paraphrasing
See page 180.

CRITICAL THINKING STRATEGY:
Evaluating
See page 189.

CRITICAL THINKING STRATEGY:
Classifying
See page 187.

4. **Pair Work.** Take turns retelling the stories in your own words. Use your chart from Activity 3 for information.

5. **Journal Writing.** Which story did you like best? Why? Write about it in your journal. Then share ideas with your classmates.

6. **Pair Work.** A descriptive paragraph draws a picture in words. Reread one of the paragraphs about customs. What picture do you see? Tell your partner about it. Let your partner guess the custom.

Example:

I see an older man standing in a room. His hands are wrinkled, his hair is gray and his eyes sparkle. He is holding a cake over his head, as though it were a hat. Several children are walking around him and looking up at the cake. Everyone is laughing.

7. **Group Work.** Study this picture. Imagine you are there and answer the questions below. Choose one person to write your group's answers on another piece of paper. Then compare answers with your classmates.

- What do you see?

- What do you hear?

- What do you smell?

8. Writing Assignment. In writing, tell your classmates about one of your family customs. Here are some steps you can follow:

   a. In your journal, brainstorm a list of customs in your family. Read your list to a partner. Listen to your partner's list. (This might help you to think of more ideas.)

   b. Choose one of the customs on your list. Quickwrite about it in your journal.

   c. Reread your quickwriting. Underline the ideas you like.

   d. Tell a partner about this custom. Answer any questions your partner has.

   e. In writing, describe your family custom.

   f. Read Around. Get together with a group of classmates. Take turns reading each other's writing.

   g. Place your writing in your writing folder.

CHAPTER THREE

Comparing Families

✱ ★ ✱ ★ ✱ ★ ✱ ✱

WRITING STRATEGY:
*Making a
Venn Diagram*
See page 175.

1. **Pair Work.** Talk to a partner. Find out how your families are the same and different. Write your ideas on a Venn diagram.

Example:

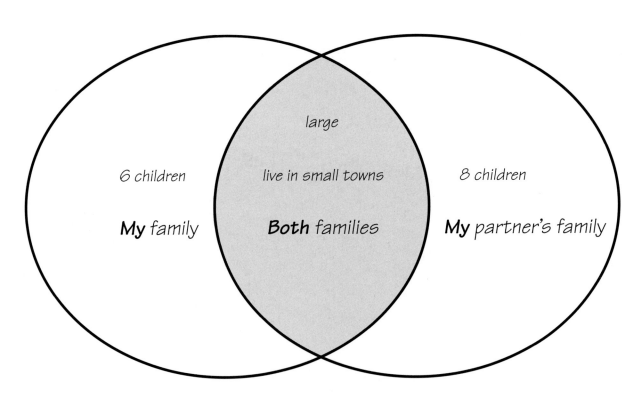

large

6 children   live in small towns   8 children

My family   **Both** families   **My** partner's family

Tell another pair of students about the ideas on your Venn diagram.

Example: My family is large, and so is Mahmoud's.
Both of our families live in small towns.
My parents have 6 children, but Mahmoud's parents have 8.

2. **On Your Own.** Take notes in the chart below as you read pages 124–125. Tell about each of the families in the reading.

❋☆❋☆❋☆❋☆❋

READING STRATEGY:
*Taking Notes
in a Chart*
See page 183.

Family	Description
the author and her family	*lived in a house trailer, parents divorced*
Linda and her family	
Carol and her family	
kids in the movies	

Compare charts with your classmates.

This passage is the introduction to a book called Free To Be…A Family. *This book is a collection of stories that explore the many different ways of being a family in today's world. In her introduction to the book, the author Gloria Steinem shares her ideas about what a family is.*

from Free to Be…A Family
by Gloria Steinem

I always thought my family was different from other families. For one thing, we lived and traveled in a house trailer most of the winters before I was ten, so I learned to read and write from my parents and my older sister instead of going to school.

For another thing, my parents separated and divorced[1] when I was about eleven. I don't remember feeling sad about that fact—I knew they both would be happier, and I knew they loved me no matter where we lived—but movies told me you were supposed to feel bad if your parents got divorced.

Finally, my very gentle and kind mother was sick a lot of the time, so I often cooked her meals and took care of her instead of the other way around.

All of this made me feel odd.

So, I envied my friend Linda who went to school like everybody else, and who lived with her mother and brother in a little apartment above a movie theater. How great to see your friends everyday, and to go downstairs to a movie whenever you wanted.

And I envied my friend Carol who lived in a neat little row house with her sister and brother and parents. How great to have your meals cooked for you and your clothes ironed for you, and to live in a house where you could invite your friends!

Most of all, I envied the kids in Hollywood movies who had fresh strawberries for breakfast, clean clothes every day, birthday parties, and even horses to ride.

Years later, I talked to my grown-up friends and realized something very interesting. Linda said she had felt funny because her mother was a widow and they didn't live in a real house. Carol had

---

1 **divorced** ended a marriage officially

124

been a little ashamed because her father went to work in overalls[2] and didn't speak English very well. Both of them envied me because I didn't have to go to school all the time, I had traveled to lots of different places, and I made up my own rules because I was being my own mother.

All of us felt a little bad because we didn't live the way that kids did in the movies.

Well, the first thing this book can do is show that movies and other made-up images[3] aren't always right or real. Neither are all of our ideas about what a "real family" is. If we feel loved and supported for being special and unique,[4] if we have enough food and a warm, dry place to live, if we have people we love and feel close to, then we are probably in a real family. It doesn't matter whether it is one we got born into, or one we chose, or one that chose us, or one that came together because people who already had families loved each other and decided to blend[5] them into one.

Of course, there will always be problems, because problems are things that make us stronger tomorrow than we were today. That's how we grow. This book tells us that, too.

But no one way of living can be right for everybody. How boring the world would be if we were all alike! This book can help us feel good about ourselves and help us use our unique families to become the very best people we can be.

---

2 **overalls**   a type of work pants worn over other clothes to protect them from dirt
3 **images**   pictures in your mind
4 **unique**   one of a kind
5 **blend**   put together or combine

CRITICAL THINKING
STRATEGY:
Comparing
See page 188.

READING STRATEGY:
Using Context
See page 184.

3. **Pair Work.** Choose two of the families from your chart in Activity 2. Tell how they are the same and different. Take turns giving examples.

    Examples: *The author's family moved around a lot but Linda's family didn't.*

    Linda went to school but the author didn't.

4. **On Your Own.** Find these words in the passage. Use context to guess the meaning of each word. Then use the word in a sentence about yourself.

    a. Paragraph 3: took care of

    My definition: _____

    Sentence: _____

    b. Paragraph 5: envied

    My definition: _____

    Sentence: _____

    c. Paragraph 8: ashamed

    My definition: _____

    Sentence: _____

    d. Paragraph 8: made up

    My definition: _____

    Sentence: _____

    Read your sentences to the class.

5. **Journal Writing.** What is your reaction to the reading on pages 124–125? Write your ideas in your journal. Here are some questions you might think about:

- What is the author's definition of a "real family"?

- Do you agree or disagree with her definition? Why?

- Did you ever wish your family were different? If so, how?

When you have finished writing, choose one of your ideas to read to the class.

CRITICAL THINKING
STRATEGY:
Analyzing
See page 185.

6. **Writing Assignment.** How are families alike and different? Explore this question by comparing two families you know well. Here are some suggestions to help you get started:

a. Choose two families you know well.

b. Collect ideas about the two families. Try one or more of these strategies:

- Make a cluster diagram.

- Quickwrite about each family.

- Take notes in chart form.

- Tell a partner about the families.

- Write questions and answers about each family.

- Make a Venn diagram comparing the two families.

c. In writing, tell your classmates about the two families.

d. Exchange papers with a partner. Read each other's papers.

e. Place your writing in your writing folder.

CHAPTER FOUR

Defining Family

1. **Class Work.** Think of someone you know. Who does this person live with? Choose one person to write your ideas on the board.

   Example: *My sister lives with a female friend.*

   In your opinion, which of these "domestic arrangements" is a family? Why?

2. **Pair Work.** Some experts say that families are built out of powerful commitments—promises or obligations. What do you think these commitments are? Make a list.

   to protect each other

   _____

   _____

   _____

   _____

   _____

   _____

   _____

   _____

   _____

   _____

   _____

Read your list to the class.

3. **On Your Own.** Read the first sentence of each paragraph on pages 130–131. Then write a question about each sentence. Ask something you really want to find out. Read your questions to the class and together predict answers.

⟨✳✶✳✦✳✶✳✦✳⟩
READING STRATEGY:
Asking Questions
See page 178.

Paragraph	Question	Text answer
1	How has it changed?	
2		
3		
4		
5		
6		
7		
8		
9		
10		
11		
12		

4. **On Your Own.** As you read the magazine article, look for answers to your questions from Activity 3. Add the answers to your chart.

What Is a Family?

by Bernard Gavzer

The definition of family in America has changed radically in the last few decades. For one thing, the traditional family—two parents, a father who works and a mother who raises her two or three children at home—is waning. At the same time, one-parent families are becoming more common.

We also see new types of domestic arrangements. Some people say they are families, while others argue that they are not. Who is right? What is a "family" anyway? And what values should a family, any family, strive for?

No matter what the composition, strong families have certain things in common: they are built out of powerful commitments, say the experts. These commitments are to nurture and protect the young, while preparing them to join society; and to protect and support the well-being of the elderly.

These two goals are prized among people who differ in race, religion, wealth, heritage, and culture. And they are shared by people whose lifestyles are both traditional and non-traditional, says Thomas F. Coleman, director of the Family Diversity Project in Los Angeles.

Doris Cone, 70, and her husband, Don, 71, of Baywood Park, California, typify a traditional arrangement. They have been married for 50 years. Two of their three children are married and have children of their own. Don Cone gave up a possible career as a corporate executive in order to build a strong family.

"It was clear in my company that if you were going to get ahead, you had to give your life to the company," says Don Cone. "But I put my family, my work with the Boy Scouts, and the church ahead of everything else."

Patricia Conway, 41, a teacher in Portland, Oregon, and James Brunkow, 42, a chimney sweep, are not married. But they've been together for 11 years and have four children. Their family is the center of their life. Their kitchen is usually crowded with children doing homework and the family spends a lot of time together.

Yet Conway and Brunkow are not legally a family. The U.S. Census Bureau defines a "family" as those related by blood, marriage, or adoption. Failing to meet that definition, unmarried couples can have problems, from getting health insurance to filing joint income-tax returns.

"Being married is not the issue," says Brunkow. "The commitment I make to Patricia and the kids is one I make freely. We are choosing to live in this fashion. Because we do, it doesn't mean that we should be denied any of the benefits that normally exist between people who are married."

Dmitri Belser, 34, and Tom While, 37, who are homosexuals, call themselves a family too. The two have accepted the responsibilities of a marriage and family. However, they cannot get the benefits of one because the law does not recognize such arrangements as "marriages."

"We are a family," insists Belser. "We have two sons. The adoption papers name us both as parents. But the state won't recognize us as a couple, even though everything we have is held in common."

For some people, these non-traditional arrangements are not real families. But Linda Walker, a single mother who is raising her four young children and two young nieces, wants to know how anyone could say they are not a family.

This selection was taken from Parade Magazine.

5. **Pair Work.** Share any answers you found to your questions in Activity 3. Show where in the reading you found the answers. Then report what you learned to the class.

6. **Pair Work.** What family commitments does this writer identify? List them below. Are they the same as or different from the commitments that you listed in Activity 2?

_____

_____

_____

_____

_____

Compare lists with your classmates.

7. **Journal Writing.** Describe one of the domestic arrangements in the reading. What questions does it raise for you? Explore these questions as you write in your journal.

8. **Group Work.** Follow the instructions below.

   a. Take turns describing the four types of domestic arrangements mentioned in this article.

   b. In your opinion, which of these domestic arrangements are families? Why? Choose one person to report your group's answer to the class.

9. **Group Work.** Find the words below in the reading. Use context to guess the meaning of each word. Then answer the questions. Choose one person to report your group's answers to the class.

READING STRATEGY: *Using Context* See page 184.

a. Paragraph 1: waning

Definition: _____

Why do you think the traditional family is *waning* in the United

States? _____

_____

b. Paragraph 3: nurture

Definition: _____

How do parents *nurture* their children? Give an example. _____

_____

c. Paragraph 5: traditional

Definition: _____

What is a *traditional* family? Give another example. _____

_____

d. Paragraph 6: get ahead

Definition: _____

What do you think a corporate executive has to do to *get ahead*

in the job? _____

_____

10. **Writing Assignment.** Describe one person's domestic arrangement and explain why you think it is or is not a family. You can follow the steps below for more specific suggestions.

✺✮✺✮✺✮✺✮✺

WRITING STRATEGY:
Collecting Information
See page 170.

a. Interview someone outside of class—someone you know well. Find out about this person's domestic arrangement. Here are some questions you might want to ask in your interview:

- *Who do you live with now?*

- *What do you like and dislike about this arrangement?*

- *What do you do for each other?*

- *What do you share?*

- *What commitments, if any, do you have?*

b. Take careful notes as you talk to this person. You might want to collect several direct quotes (the person's exact words) to use in your writing.

Examples:

- *lives with a friend*
  "We share expenses."

- *likes having someone to eat with*
  "We usually eat dinner together. I like that."

- *help each other with problems*
  "We talk a lot. She tells me her problems and I tell her mine."

c. Reread your notes. Circle the ideas you might want to include in your writing.

d. In writing, describe the domestic arrangement to your class-mates. Include some quotes from the person you interviewed. Then explain why this domestic arrangement is or is not a family in your opinion.

e. Read Around. Get together with a group of classmates. Take turns reading each other's writing.

f. Place your writing in your writing folder.

UNIT FOUR
Final Project

For your final project, choose one of your first drafts from Unit 4 to revise. Here are some questions you might ask yourself as you revise your writing:

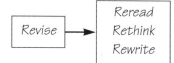

Revise → Reread Rethink Rewrite

- Do you "hook" your reader right away?

- Do you give your reader enough information?

- Do you use details to explain and support important ideas?

As you revise your paper, pay special attention to your concluding paragraph. Remember that your conclusion is the "end" of your piece of writing. It is your last chance to tell your reader something. Try experimenting with different ways of writing your conclusion:

- Ask a question, directly or indirectly. Leave the reader thinking. (See "What Is a Family?," pages 130–131.)

- Summarize your important ideas.

- Solve the problem or unravel the mystery. (See "Two Brothers," pages 112–113.)

- State your most important idea. (See "Free to Be…A Family," pages 124–125.)

For more ideas on writing conclusions, look over the next two pages. On page 136, you can see some different ways that students using *The Multicultural Workshop* wrote conclusions. On page 137, you can read one writer's thoughts on writing conclusions.

These examples show different ways that students using *The Multicultural Workshop* concluded some of their writing.

❶

…My parents have responsibilities to us, and my brother and I have our own responsibilities to our parents. That is the way of life. If it was not for responsibility, who could imagine what this society would be?

(the conclusion to a piece on families by Tien Thuy Le)

❷

…Sometimes I remember with sadness those days when I was a child, and my wish is to return to the past. Those days were the happiest of my life.

(the last line of an autobiographical essay by Maria A. Castro)

❸

…I think that my friend's domestic arrangement is very good. The parents have time for their children's education, and everyone in the family can help each other. I really like that.

(conclusion to a paragraph about families by Thanh Dang)

❹

…On one occasion, some friends were scoffing at a poor girl and Ruth asked them, "Why are you laughing at that girl?" She explained that nobody had the right to laugh at other people. People should be known for the values they hold.

(conclusion to an essay about a friend by Diane Echenique Janowsky)

Writing Conclusions

Concluding an essay can seem silly. You ask yourself, "What more is there to write? I've said all that I want to say." I used to feel the same way until a teacher told me that a conclusion is the ideal place to leave the reader thinking.

Leave the reader thinking.

I believe that conclusions work best when they summarize the main points **and** add something extra. If my readers are thinking about my ideas after they finish reading, I know my concluding paragraph is good. Sometimes, I ask a question to make readers rethink what I've said. Other times, I try to connect the topic to my readers personally.

Summarize the main points and....

If the subject is serious, talking about the "big picture" can work well. I can show that a particular topic is universal. If, for example, the rights of older people is the topic, I might say that (with some luck) the readers will be old someday. Wouldn't my readers like to know that their rights will be protected when they reach 60 or 70?

Show that the topic is universal.

For me, it's usually late at night when I reach my conclusion. I am tired and losing my concentration. If I'm really exhausted, I save the concluding paragraph for the next day. "Sleeping[1]" on my writing helps me think more clearly. The next day, my conclusion is easier to write. My mind is clear, and I'm ready to tackle[2] that final important paragraph.

"Sleep" on your writing.

—*Amanda Buege*

ABOUT THE AUTHOR
Amanda Buege is a graduate student at the University of New Orleans. She wrote her thoughts for students using *The Multicultural Workshop.*

---

1 **sleeping on something**   waiting until the next day to continue
2 **tackle**   do something difficult

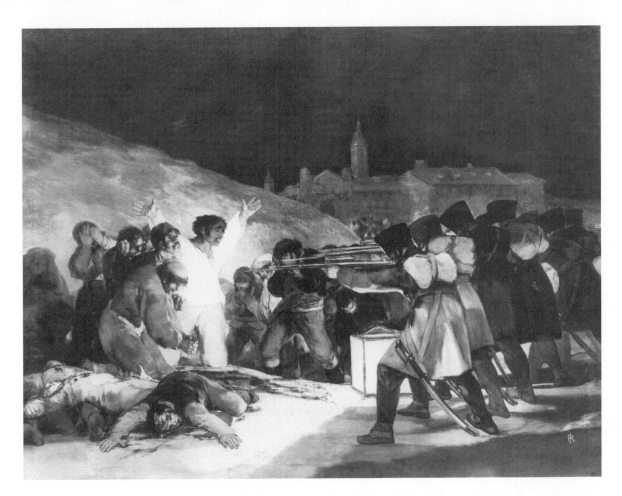

Francisco Goya, *3 May 1808*

UNIT FIVE
Conflict

In this unit you will read four selections related to the theme of conflict.

• What does the word *conflict* mean to you?

CHAPTER ONE

Resolving Conflict

1. Group Work. Read these definitions of conflict and answer the questions below.

> **conflict** / *n* ❶ disagreement; argument; quarrel: *The two political parties have been in conflict since the election.* ❷ war; battle, struggle: *Armed conflict could start at any time. There is a possibility of a serious conflict between the two countries.*
>
> — adapted from *Longman Dictionary of American English*

a. In the world today, where is armed conflict taking place?

_____

_____

_____

✹★✹★✹★✹★✹

**CRITICAL THINKING
STRATEGY:
*Analyzing***
See page 185.

---

b. What might cause the conflicts below? List several ideas.

a war between two countries

   disagreement over land
_____

_____

an argument between a husband and wife

_____

_____

a quarrel between two friends

_____

_____

Choose one student to report your group's ideas from *a* and *b* above.

2. **Group Work.** Read the first two frames of the cartoon on the next
   page. Answer these questions:

   a. What's the cause of the conflict?

   _____

   _____

   b. How do you think the conflict might be resolved, or cleared up?
       Predict three possible ways.

       They might get into a fight and the winner will cross the bridge first.
       _____

       _____

       _____

       _____

       _____

       _____

READING STRATEGY:
Predicting
See page 181.

   Choose one student to report your group's ideas to the class.

3. **Class Work.** Read the rest of the cartoon to find out how the conflict is resolved.

Animal Crackers

by Roger Bollen

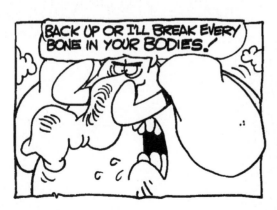

4. **Pair Work.** Read the cartoon aloud as a dialogue. Experiment with your tone of voice.

5. **Pair Work.** Rewrite the dialogue in the cartoon on page 142. Resolve the conflict in a different way. Then read your dialogue to the class.

6. **Class Work.** How does the elephant in the cartoon use body language (facial expressions and body movements) to show anger? What are some other ways people show anger? List your ideas on the board.

7. **Group Work.** What do you think the people in these photographs are saying or thinking? Choose one person to record your group's ideas. Then compare ideas with your classmates.

> CRITICAL THINKING
> STRATEGY:
> *Analyzing*
> See page 142.

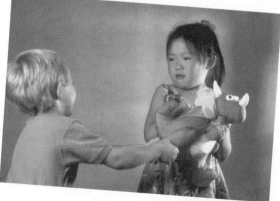

■✱■✱■✱■✱■

WRITING STRATEGY:
Quickwriting
See page 176.

■✱■✱■✱■✱■

WRITING STRATEGY:
Listing Ideas
See page 172.

8. **Journal Writing.** Quickwrite about a disagreement you had with someone. Here are some questions you might think about:

- What did you disagree about?
- What did you do?
- How was the conflict resolved?
- Would you handle the conflict in the same way today?

9. **Writing Assignment.** Write a dialogue in which two people disagree about something. Follow the steps below for more specific suggestions.

a. Group Work. What might these pairs of people disagree about? List your ideas on another piece of paper.

Husband and Wife	Girlfriend and Boyfriend	Two Friends
how to discipline the children		
how to spend money		

b. On Your Own. Quickwrite about one of the conflicts from your list above. Here are some questions you might think about:

- Who are the two people?
- Where are they?
- What do they say to each other?
- What body language do they use?
- How do they resolve the conflict?

c. Use ideas from your quickwriting to write a dialogue between the two people.

d. Add an introduction to your dialogue.

- Identify the characters.
- Describe the setting. (Be specific.)
- Introduce the problem and give any important background information.

e. Ask two classmates to practice reading your dialogue aloud. Suggest appropriate body language to use. Read your introduction to the class and have the two students role-play your dialogue for the class.

f. Place your writing in your writing folder.

CHAPTER TWO

Bringing People Together

1. **Class Work.** What are some ways you can get to know people from different cultures? List your ideas.

   travel
   _____

   _____

   _____

   _____

   _____

   Which way do you think is the best? Why?

2. **Group Work.** Read the title and the first paragraph of the magazine article on the next page. What is your answer to the question in the first paragraph? Why? Write your group's response below.

   _____

   _____

   _____

   _____

   _____

   Choose one student to report your group's response.

   > **READING STRATEGY:**
   > *Previewing*
   > See page 181.

3. **On Your Own.** Read the whole article to compare answers from Activity 2.

Aiming for Peace

by Scott Brodeur

Can a simple game of hoops[1] bring together two totally different cultures and communities?

People in Brooklyn, New York, think so. And they have some results to prove it.

For years, Hasidic Jews and African-Americans have lived side by side with one another in the Crown Heights section of Brooklyn. But they have never bothered to learn much about one another.

Last year, violent riots broke out after a young African-American was killed by a Hasidic driver. Soon after, a Hasidic man was stabbed[2] to death.

The two groups became bitter enemies. That's when community leaders started CURE, a program to bring together teens from both groups. CURE stands for Communication, Understanding, Respect, and Education.

A central part of CURE is the Peace Games. In the Peace Games, Hasidic and African-American teens meet on the basketball court. The teams consist of youths from both communities. To win a game, these teens must learn how to play together and get along.

"Before, we would just say Hasidic people were different without trying to understand why," says Sean Joe, 24. "It was surprising to find out we had things in common—like basketball, music, and a love of good food."

---

1 **hoops**   basketball
2 **stabbed to death**   killed with a knife

146

At first, Yudi Simon had his doubts. He and his father had been attacked by a group of Crown Heights youths during the riots. His father had been stabbed in the leg. So Yudi, 16, wasn't sure what to expect.

"As soon as I started to play, though, I saw how effective basketball was," he says. "In order to play basketball, you have to trust your teammates. You need to use teamwork. These are the same skills you need in order to get along."

Since the first basketball games were played, the groups have gotten together to paint a mural, plant trees, and even form an interracial rap group.

The results have been good. The violence has stopped. And Yudi says he meets kids from the program all the time.

"You see someone you know from playing basketball, and you go say hello and talk," he says. "That never happened here before."

This selection was taken from Scholastic Action Magazine.

WRITING STRATEGY:
*Developing a
Point of View*
See page 170.

4. **Journal Writing.** Imagine that you are Sean Joe or Yudi Simon (mentioned in the article). Tell about your experience with the Peace Games. Here are some questions you might think about:

• Where do you live?

• How did you feel when the riots broke out in your community?

• How did you feel about the people in your community?

• What happened during the Peace Games?

• How do you feel now about the people in your community?

Choose one of your ideas to read to the class.

5. **Group Work.**

a. Why do you think the community leaders chose basketball to bring the teenagers together? List your ideas.

_____

_____

_____

_____

_____

_____

_____

_____

WRITING STRATEGY:
*Collecting
Information*
See page 170.

b. Get together with another group. Interview the students in this group. Find an activity, interest, or hobby that they all have in common.

c. In your group, plan an activity or event to help these students get to know each other. Keep in mind your list of ideas above.

d. Describe your plan to the class.

6. On Your Own. Words often have more than one meaning. Read these sentences from the article. Use context to choose the correct meaning of each **boldfaced** word from the list of dictionary definitions. Compare answers with your classmates.

READING STRATEGY:
Using Context
See page 184.

  a. *For years, Hasidic Jews and African-Americans have lived side by side with one another in the Crown Heights section of Brooklyn. But they have never **bothered** to learn much about one another.*

Definition: _____

bother / *v* ❶ to cause to be nervous; annoy or trouble, esp. in little ways: *I'm busy. Don't bother me./ That's what bothers me most. / (polite) I'm sorry to bother you, but can you tell me the time?* ❷ to cause inconvenience or trouble to oneself: *Don't bother to call.*

  b. *Last year, violent **riots** broke out after a young African-American was killed by a Hasidic driver.*

Definition: _____

riot / *n* ❶ a lot of violent actions, noisy behavior, etc., by a number of people together: *The army was called in to put down a riot./ The football players ran riot* (=became violent and uncontrollable) *after the defeat of their team.* ❷ *informal* a very funny and successful occasion or person: *I hear the new show is a riot; let's go and see it!*

  c. *The two groups became **bitter** enemies. That's when community leaders started CURE, a program to bring together teens from both groups.*

Definition: _____

bitter / *adj* ❶ having a sharp, biting taste, like beer or black coffee without sugar ❷ (of cold, wind, etc.) very sharp, keen, cutting, biting, etc.: *a bitter winter wind* ❸ filled with or caused by hate, anger, sorrow, or other unpleasant feelings: *It was a bitter disappointment to him when he failed his examination.*

d. *The teams consist of youths from both communities. To win a game, these teens must learn how to play together and **get along**.*

Definition: _____

get along / v adv ❶ (of people) to move away; leave: *I have to be getting along now.* ❷ (of people and activities) to advance; go well: *How is your work getting along?* ❸ to continue (often in spite of difficulties): *We can get along without your help.* ❸ (of people) to have a friendly relationship (with another or each other): *Do you get along well with your aunt?*

—definitions adapted from *Longman Dictionary of American English*

7. **Pair Work.** The word *CURE* is an acronym. It is formed from the first letter of each word in the name of the program described in the reading: **C**ommunication, **U**nderstanding, **R**espect, and **E**ducation. Do you know the meaning of the acronyms below?

NATO: _____

UNESCO: _____

SEATO: _____

Compare ideas with your classmates.

READING STRATEGY:
Summarizing
See page 183.

---

8. **Writing Assignment.** Write a summary of the article on pages 146–147 for someone outside of class. Here are some ideas to help you get started:

a. Pair Work. Newspaper reporters learn to ask a set of questions when they report an event. These questions are sometimes called the five Ws: *Who? What? When? Where? Why?* (and sometimes *How?*).

Imagine that you are a newspaper reporter. Take turns asking and answering questions to check your understanding of the Peace Games.

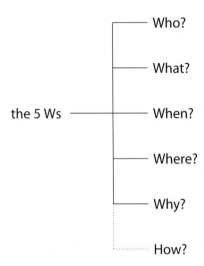

the 5 Ws
- Who?
- What?
- When?
- Where?
- Why?
- How?

b. A summary reduces a long text to a short one. It gives the main ideas, but skips unnecessary details. Use the answers to your questions to write a summary of the article for someone outside of your class.

c. Read Around. Get together with a group of students. Take turns reading each other's summary.

d. Place your writing in your writing folder.

CHAPTER THREE

Experiencing Discrimination

1. **Class Work.** Read the statements below. Who are the "victims" of discrimination, or unfair treatment?

   a. Our company hires only people under forty-five.

   people over 45
   _____

   b. This is a segregated club. Only white people can join.

   _____

   c. We can't hire people who are overweight.

   _____

   d. This job is too hard for women.

   _____

   e. He didn't get the job because he has a foreign accent.

   _____

2. **Journal Writing.** Quickwrite about discrimination for ten minutes. Here are some questions you might want to think about:

   • Have you ever been discriminated against? How did you feel?

   • Have you known someone who was discriminated against? How?

   • Why does discrimination exist?

3. Pair Work. Read the information below. Then write a caption for each of the photographs.

> Before the modern civil rights movement, many places in the United States had laws that segregated, or separated, black and white Americans. These laws forced black Americans to use separate schools, restrooms, restaurants, and other public facilities. Usually the facilities for black people were not as good as the facilities for white people.

Read your captions to the class.

_____

_____

_____

CRITICAL THINKING STRATEGY: *Analyzing* See page 185.

❋ ✭ ❋ ✭ ❋ ✭ ❋ ✭ ❋

READING STRATEGY:
Asking Questions
See page 178.

4. **Group Work.** Read the title of the newspaper article on the next page. What questions does the title raise for you? List them. For each question, suggest an answer.

Question: _____ *Who are the "Yooups"?* _____

_____

Possible answer: _____

_____

Question: _____

_____

Possible answer: _____

_____

Question: _____

_____

Possible answer: _____

_____

Share your questions and predictions with your classmates.

5. **Group Work.** Read the newspaper article and look for answers to your questions.

'Yooups' learned bitter discrimination lesson

ATLANTA (AP)—Seventy-five students volunteered to be victims of discrimination. They knew what was going to happen, but they weren't prepared for what it felt like.

The seventy-five students at Sandy Springs Middle School were labeled "yooups" (YOu are one of the grOUP) for one day. This experiment was supposed to help them understand what it was like to be black in America before the civil rights movement.

"The entire experiment was explained to them in advance by their homeroom teachers and they knew what was going to happen," said David Rector, who organized the experiment at the predominantly[1] white school in suburban Atlanta. "But they weren't really ready for what happened. That's the whole point. It's something you have to live to understand."

The students—from different ethnic backgrounds—wore white armbands identifying them as yooups.

They were jeered[2] by other students, forced to use the "yooups only" water fountain and restrooms, segregated during lunch and class, and discriminated against by teachers who blamed them for the misconduct of other students.

The yooups also rode in the back of the bus on the the way to school and entered the building through a specially marked "yooups only" entrance.

"This morning they thought it was going to be a fun activity," Rector said Tuesday after the experiment was over. "But there was a noticeable change as the day progressed."

"I could see the apprehension building in the yooups. As the day wore on, they began to ask questions about being physically and verbally abused," he said.

"It's terrible," Brant Petree said. "Everybody makes fun of you. It makes you feel bad, hurts your feelings."

"It was real hard work," said John Tyson. "Some of us aren't used to being told to sit in the back of the room, line up last, eat a different dessert, get snapped at[3] by the teachers."

By the end of the day, Rector said the yooups told him they had "learned a great deal about their fellow students and teachers. It was not a pleasant experience for many of them."

---

1 **predominantly**   mostly; mainly
2 **jeered**   laughed at rudely; made fun of
3 **snapped at**   spoken to angrily

READING STRATEGY:
Scanning
See page 182.

6. **Group Work.** How were the "yooups" discriminated against? Look back over the article quickly to find the ways. List them below.

They had to wear white armbands.

_____

_____

_____

_____

Read your answers to the class.

7. **Group Work.** Discuss the questions below. Choose one person to record your group's answers. Choose another person to report your answers to the class.

a. The "yooups" experiment is one way to teach young people about discrimination. What are some other ways? List your ideas.

Example: *reading stories about discrimination*

_____

_____

b. In your opinion, what's the best way to teach young people about discrimination? Why?

WRITING STRATEGY:
Brainstorming
See page 169.

8. **On Your Own.** Find these words in the article. Use the context to guess the meaning of each word. Then answer the questions.

a. Paragraph 1: volunteered

My definition: _____

Would you *volunteer* to be a "yooup" for a day? Why or why not?

_____

_____

READING STRATEGY:
Using Context
See page 184.

b. Paragraph 5: misconduct

My definition: _____

What's an example of student *misconduct* in school? _____

_____

c. Paragraph 8: apprehension

My definition: _____

What makes you feel *apprehensive*? _____

_____

d. Paragraph 9: makes fun of

My definition: _____

How do you think students *made fun of* the "yooups"? What did

they do or say? _____

_____

9. **Writing Assignment.** Write about the "yooups" experiment for someone outside of class to read. Read the steps below for more specific suggestions.

a. What's your reaction to the "yooups" experiment? Quickwrite for ten minutes. Here are some questions you might think about:

• How did the experiment affect students?

• Do you think the results were positive or negative? Why?

• Do you think students learned a valuable lesson? Why or why not?

b. Compare reactions with a classmate.

> **CRITICAL THINKING STRATEGY:**
> *Evaluating*
> See page 189.

c. In writing, evaluate the "yooups" experiment for a friend outside of class. Here are some ideas you might want to include:

- Summarize the experiment. Tell briefly what it was about.

- Tell what you think was positive. Give specfic examples.

- Tell what you think was negative. Give specific ideas.

- Give your advice. Tell if you think other schools should try this experiment.

d. Ask a friend outside of class to read your paper.

e. Place your writing in your writing folder.

CHAPTER FOUR

Analyzing War

1. **Class Work.** On the board, make a chart like the one below. Take turns telling about a war that took place in your country.

Example:

Where?	When?	Who?	Why?
United States	1860s	North vs. South	disagreement about slavery different lifestyles and economies

❀★✿★❀★✿★❀★✿

WRITING STRATEGY:
Taking Notes in a Chart
See page 177.

2. **Group Work.** For what reasons, if any, would you be willing to fight in a war? List your reasons. Then share them with the class.

to protect my home

_____

_____

_____

_____

_____

_____

_____

❀★✿★❀★✿★❀★✿

CRITICAL THINKING STRATEGY:
Analyzing
See page 185.

3. **Class Work.** Listen as your teacher reads the following poem aloud. Then read it aloud with a partner.

Nationality

I have grown past hate and bitterness,
I see the world as one;
Yet, though I can no longer hate,
My son is still my son.
     All men at God's round table sit,
     And all men must be fed;
     But this loaf in my hand,
     This loaf is my son's bread.

—Mary Gilmore

4. **Journal Writing.** Explore your reaction to the poem as you write in your journal. Here are some questions you can think about:

   • Do you like this poem? Why or why not?

   • What do you know about the speaker in the poem?

   • Do you think this person is for or against war? Why?

   When you have finished writing, choose one idea to read to your classmates.

5. **Group Work.** Choose one person to record your group's answers to the questions below.

   • Why do you think the poem is titled "Nationality"?

   • Why do you think the last four lines are indented?

   Choose another person to report your group's ideas to the class.

6. **Pair Work.**

   a. In what ways might a war change your life and your beliefs? List your ideas.

   I might have to leave my home.

   _____

   _____

   _____

   _____

   _____

   _____

   _____

   _____

   _____

CRITICAL THINKING
STRATEGY:
Interpreting
See page 190.

CRITICAL THINKING
STRATEGY:
Analyzing
See page 185.

b. The writer Simone Weil defines war as "the transformation of man into a thing." What do you think she means? Give an illustration.

_____

_____

_____

_____

_____

c. Get together with another pair and share ideas from *a* and *b* above. Then tell what this picture means to you.

Juan Genoves,
One, Two, Seven, Seven

7. **Pair Work.** Listen as your teacher reads the following poem aloud. Then take turns reading it aloud to a partner.

(Untitled)

They held up a stone.
    I said, 'Stone.'
Smiling they said, 'Stone.'
They showed me a tree.
    I said, 'Tree.'
Smiling they said, 'Tree.'
They shed a man's blood.
    I said, 'Blood.'
Smiling they said, 'Paint.'
They shed a man's blood.
    I said, 'Blood.'
Smiling they said, 'Paint.'

—Dannie Abse, adapted from the
Hebrew of Amir Gilboa

❊ ✭ ❊ ✭ ❊ ✭ ❊ ✭ ❊

READING STRATEGY:
Asking Questions
See page 178.

8. **Group Work.** Write three opinion-questions about the poem. (Opinion-questions do not have right or wrong answers.) Exchange questions with another group and answer their questions.

   Example: *Why doesn't the poem have a title?*

   Read the questions and your answers to the class.

9. **Writing Assignment.**

   a. Choose the quotation below that interests you most:

      • "Sometime they'll give a war and nobody will come."
        —Carl Sandburg

      • "In time of war the first casualty is truth." —Boake Carter

      • "War is fear cloaked in courage." —William Westmoreland

      • "There are no warlike peoples—just warlike leaders."
        —Ralphe Bunche

❊ ✭ ❊ ✭ ❊ ✭ ❊ ✭ ❊

**CRITICAL THINKING
STRATEGY:**
Interpreting
See page 190.

   b. What's your reaction to the quotation? Quickwrite in your journal for five minutes.

   c. Read the quotation to a classmate. Read several ideas from your quickwriting. Listen to your classmate's reaction.

   d. Choose a form in which to present your reaction to the quotation. Here are a few suggestions:

      • Write a poem.

      • Write a letter to the author of the quotation.

      • Write a dialogue between yourself and the author of the quotation.

UNIT FIVE
Final Project

For your final project, choose one of your rough drafts from Unit 5 to revise. Your revised writing will be collected in a booklet for your classmates to read. Your teacher will also use your revised writing to help you evaluate your progress.

As you revise your writing, focus on the arrangement (organization) of ideas. You might ask yourself these questions:

- At the beginning of your writing, do you make your topic clear? Can your reader understand what you are writing about?

- Do you "build up" your important ideas with details? Do you explain your ideas to your reader?

- Are your ideas in the best order for your readers?

Use a chart like this to check the order of your important ideas:

Paragraph	Important Idea	Details
2	happy childhood memories	• play with friends • go to park and zoo • catch beetles

For more help on arranging your ideas, study the next three pages. On pages 166–167, you can see how one writer develops and arranges her ideas. On page 168, you can read another writer's thoughts on organizing ideas.

Read these drafts to see how one writer reorganized her writing.

First Draft

The focus is unclear.

Too many ideas and details are together.

> My childhood I lived in Vietnam. I had memories and friends. Today everything has changed.
>
> I could do everything. I went to school or went everywhere by myself. I had many friends. I could talk and joke easily because of my language. In my free time, I and my friends usually ran freely to play in the fields. When it rained, we usually took showers in the rain. When I went to high school, I wore a long, white dress. I was very happy. Today everything has changed. When I came to the U.S., I can't speak English well. I can't do many things by myself. I can't speak to everybody around me yet. I can't go everywhere by myself when I want. I am still very shy. Sometimes, I feel very sad, but sometimes I also feel happy for I am united with my family.
>
> My life had changed a lot, but I think if I am just a little more patient with myself, I will get along fine in this new society.

Third Draft:

My childhood is very interesting for I have many fond memories. I still remember my memories when I lived with my mother and brother, but today things have changed entirely.

When I lived in Vietnam, I could do everything. I could go to school, or I could go anywhere by myself. I had many friends. I talked and joked easily. In my free time, I and my friends usually ran freely to play. When it was raining, we were usually taking a shower under the rain. Sometimes, we also went to the park or zoo. The park and zoo had beautiful gardens full of flowers and shady trees. In the afternoon, when I went to the park with my friends, we walked from place to place. I saw many gorgeous butterflies. I used to run along flower-bordered walks chasing gorgeous butterflies and catching shiny beetles. We enjoyed the whole day there. These memories made up my happy childhood.

The time passed slowly. I went to school and I always saved a lot of time for my studies. I was a good student, so my mother and teachers loved me very much. In 1989, I passed into high school. I studied there for three years. All students wore uniforms. The girls wore long, white dresses. The boys wore white shirts and blue pants...[followed by three more pages about the writer's life].

—*Tien Thuy Le*

Clear focus. The reader can understand the topic.

Details are all about the writer's childhood.

Details are all about school.

One Writer's Thoughts on Organizing

Reorganize: rearrange.

Organizing my writing is a chore, similar to doing the dishes or taking out the garbage. Sometimes reorganizing is even harder than writing a first draft. Organizing is rearranging, shuffling the ideas around. As tedious as it is, though, organizing has to be done.

Keep the reader reading.

Good organization helps the reader. If sentences or paragraphs don't lead logically or smoothly into one another, the reader has to stop and start again. If this happens too many times, the reader will stop altogether. Then what's the point? Any writer writes so that other people will read.

Help the reader follow your thinking.

If an essay is organized like a sloppy collage,[1] it's easy for readers to get lost. The writer shouldn't be at war with her reader, even if she is writing about war and conflict. My readers need to find a clear path through my writing. I think of myself as a jungle guide, offering safe passage for my readers.

Keep the reader interested.

I try to organize my body paragraphs in order of their importance. If I have a "big gun,[2]" I save it for last. I always want my writing to read better as my readers continue. Paragraphs shouldn't get shorter either. My readers will notice and think I am getting tired or disinterested.

Tell the reader where you are going.

If I am writing a long essay, I'll help my readers. Sometimes I give them a road map. I'll say, "You're going to Point A, where you'll read about W and X. Then, you'll move to Point B, where you'll learn about Y and Z." If I'm a good guide, my readers can follow.

—*Amanda Buege*

ABOUT THE AUTHOR
Amanda Buege is a graduate student at the University of New Orleans. She is a writing tutor in the UNO Writing Lab, where she often works with ESL students. She wrote down her thoughts on organizing for students using *The Multicultural Workshop*.

---

1 **collage**   a picture made of objects, pictures, and/or words
2 **big gun**   something that is especially interesting, important, or surprising

Reference Guide

Writing Strategies

001 BRAINSTORMING

Brainstorming is a good way to collect ideas for writing. It is an especially useful strategy to use with a partner or with a group of people.

Follow these steps to brainstorm a set of ideas:

1. Put your writing idea on a piece of paper. This might be a word, a phrase, or a question.

2. Write down every word that comes to mind. Don't evaluate your ideas. Just think and write quickly.

Example:

Writing Idea: Growing Old

> gray hair
>
> hard of hearing
>
> tired
>
> fun
>
> slow down
>
> less work
>
> meet friends

After brainstorming, reread your list and circle the ideas you might want to use in your writing.

002 COLLECTING INFORMATION

Before you start writing, spend plenty of time collecting ideas and information. This will make your writing task much easier.

Here are a few suggestions for collecting information:

- Quickwrite about your topic for several minutes. Then look over your quickwriting for good ideas to use in your writing. (See 011 Quickwriting.)

- Write your topic on a piece of paper and then list every idea that comes to mind. Then look back over your list and choose ideas to develop. (See 005 Listing Ideas.)

- Think about your topic and write your ideas on a cluster diagram. (See 006 Making a Cluster Diagram.)

- Read other articles about your topic and take notes. Give credit if you use another writer's information and ideas in your writing.

- Interview one or more people to get their ideas on your topic.

003 DEVELOPING A POINT OF VIEW

Before you write, you need to decide through whose eyes you are going to view your topic. For example, are you going to look at your topic through the eyes of a student? a friend? a parent? a child?

Your choice of point of view shapes your writing. For example, how you "speak" as a parent is different from how you "speak" as a child. As a writer, you can write from different points of view.

004 GIVING EXAMPLES

Giving examples helps your reader to understand your ideas. It is also a good way to convince your reader that what you say is true.

Example:

My grandmother is such an active person that it is hard to believe she is 93 years old. She still drives her old Chevy though she now stays off the California freeways and keeps close to home. She reads voraciously —magazines, books, and newspapers.

Main Idea:	*My grandmother is very active.*
Examples:	*She still drives a car.*
	She reads a lot.

005 LISTING IDEAS

Listing ideas is a good strategy to use to collect ideas for writing. Simply write your topic on a piece of paper. Think about your topic and write down any important or useful ideas that come to mind. You can go back later and choose your best ideas.

Example:

Topic: Reasons for Moving to New York

• *needed a job*

• *had friends there*

• *wanted to live in a big city*

• *wanted to be near my sister*

006 MAKING A CLUSTER DIAGRAM

Making a cluster diagram is a good way to collect ideas before you start writing. Making a cluster diagram can also help you see the connection between big ideas and details.

Follow these steps to make a cluster diagram:

1. Write your topic in the center of a piece of paper. Circle it.

2. Think about your topic. What words and ideas come to mind? Write each thought in a smaller circle and connect it by a line to the circle in the center.

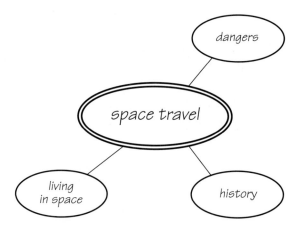

3. Think about the ideas in the smaller circles. Write down any
   ideas that come to mind and connect them to the smaller circles.

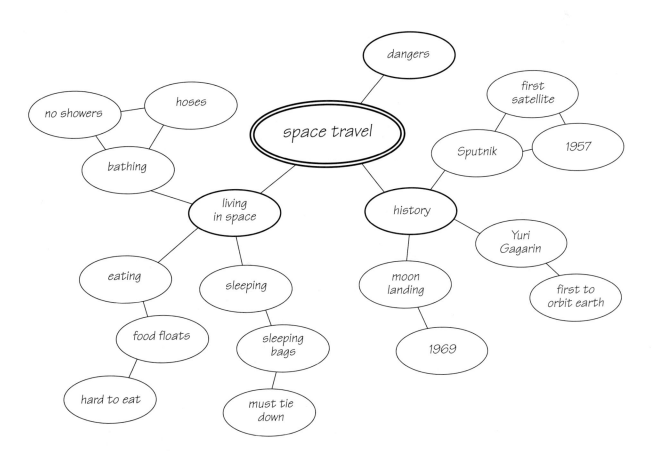

007 MAKING A TIME LINE

Making a time line is a way to organize information visually. A time line helps you to see the order of events over time. It can also help you to find examples of cause and effect.

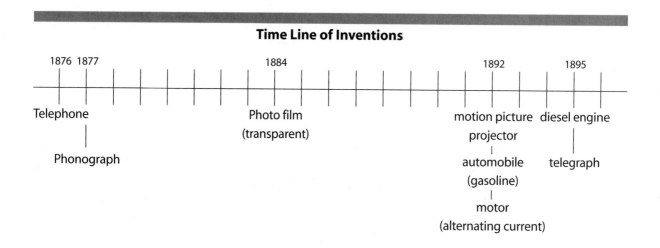

Time Line of Inventions

008 MAKING A TREE DIAGRAM

Making a tree diagram is a useful way to organize your ideas before you start writing. Before you make a tree diagram, you might want to first list ideas about your topic. Then reread your list of ideas looking for categories of information. Write these categories on your tree diagram. Then list ideas in each category.

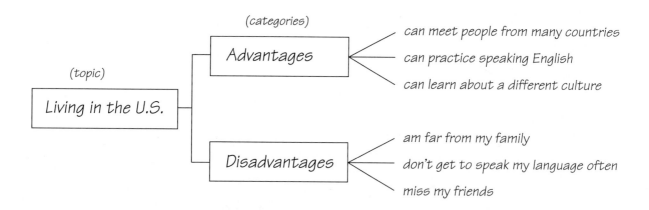

009 MAKING A VENN DIAGRAM

Use a Venn diagram to compare and contrast two things. In the center of
the diagram (where the circles overlap) list ways the two things are alike.
In the outer circles, list ways they are different. On the Venn diagram
below, one writer compares and contrasts New York and Los Angeles.

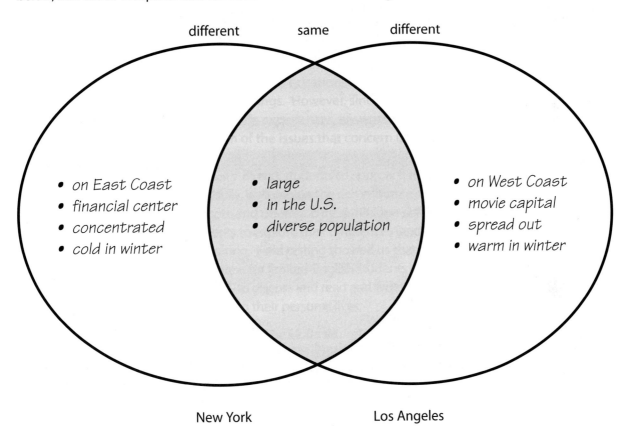

different   same   different

- on East Coast
- financial center
- concentrated
- cold in winter

- large
- in the U.S.
- diverse population

- on West Coast
- movie capital
- spread out
- warm in winter

New York   Los Angeles

010 PROVIDING DETAILS

Providing details in your writing helps your reader to create a picture from your words. Here are some ways to provide details in your writing:

• Use specific nouns.

General	Specific
car	a Toyota
a drink	a glass of lemonade
dessert	apple pie

• Use specific verbs.

General	Specific
look	stare
talk	discuss
walk	stroll

• Use "concrete" words.

Abstract	Concrete
She seemed excited.	She jumped up and down, clapping her hands and grinning from ear to ear.

011 QUICKWRITING

Quickwriting is a useful way to collect ideas for writing. Follow these steps to quickwrite:

1. Choose a topic—something you want to write about.

2. For five to ten minutes, write quickly. Don't worry about grammar or spelling. If you can't think of a word in English, write it in your native language. The important thing is to write without stopping.

3. If you can't think of anything to write, put that down or write the same word over and over again.

4. When you have finished writing, read over your ideas. Circle the ideas that you like.

Example: **Writing Topic: Growing Old**

I'm not really looking forward to growing old. Is anyone? I think about my grandmother and how difficult her life is. She's 93 now. Many of her friends are dead. She can't do a lot of things now. She has trouble walking, and she can't hear very well. But she says that inside she feels very young…. I can't think of anything to write. I can't think of anything to write. My grandmother's body is getting old, but her mind is young. She reads all of the time and she still likes to try new things. She loves to tell stories….

012 UNDERSTANDING YOUR AUDIENCE

Your audience is your reader—your classmates, a friend, your teacher, or someone you don't even know. Before you start writing, it is important to have a clear idea of who your reader is. What you say in your writing will depend in part on your reader. Try to answer these questions before you start writing:

- Who is going to read this piece of writing?
- What does my reader already know about the topic of my writing?
- Is the reader's background different from mine? How?
- What will interest my reader?
- What questions will my reader have?

013 TAKING NOTES IN A CHART

Taking notes in a chart is a good way to collect and organize ideas for writing. To make a chart, think about the kinds of information you want to collect. List this information as headings in your chart. Then add ideas and examples under each heading.

Advertisement	What message does it try to communicate to the reader?	How does it communicate the message?
Joy Perfume	*You will have interesting experiences if you wear this perfume.*	*A woman is floating on a rope ladder in the sky.*

Reading Strategies

014 ASKING QUESTIONS

Asking yourself questions is a useful strategy to use before you read, while you are reading, and after you finish reading. Asking questions can help you understand and remember ideas and information.

Before you read, study the title and any headings or pictures and then ask questions such as these:

- What is the article about?

- What do I already know about the topic?

- What do I want to find out about the topic?

While you are reading, stop frequently to ask yourself questions:

- What is this paragraph about?

- What is the writer saying here?

- What is my reaction to this paragraph?

After you finish reading, ask questions about what you read:

- What was the article about?

- What was the main idea?

- What was interesting to me?

- What did I learn?

015 FINDING MAIN IDEAS

Main ideas are the central or most important ideas that a writer wants to communicate. A story or essay may have many related ideas, but one or two ideas are usually the most important.

Sometimes the main idea is stated directly in a paragraph. The sentence that states the main idea is called the topic sentence.

Example:

<u>Success didn't change Wang's lifestyle very much</u>. Before he became the owner of a successful business, he lived simply with his wife and three children. Years later, when he was worth more than $1 billion, he still owned only two suits. And he lived in a house that many people thought was too simple for a successful businessman.

Sometimes the writer does not state the main idea directly. Instead, the reader must infer the main idea. (See 017 Making Inferences.) Here are some strategies to help you infer the main idea:

• Study the details and examples in a paragraph. Look for ways these ideas are related. Ask yourself what these ideas have in common.

• Think of a topic sentence to add to the paragraph.

Example:

In 1948, only three years after arriving in the United States, Wang earned a Ph.D. in Physics from Harvard University. After he got his Ph.D., he stayed at Harvard and worked in the Computation Laboratory. It was at this time that he invented the magnetic core. This device was a basic part of computer memory until the use of microchips in the late 1960s.

In this paragaph, each detail and example gives information about something Wang accomplished after he arrived in the United States. The examples show that he did a lot in a short period of time. From this the reader might infer the following main idea: <u>In his first years in the United States, Wang accomplished several important things.</u>

016 MAKING A STORY OUTLINE

Making a story outline helps you to focus on important information in a story. When you make a story outline, look for these main parts of a story:

Characters: Who are the people in the story?

Setting: Where and when does the story take place?

The problem or conflict: What is the central issue? What are the characters trying to do?

Important events: What happens in the story?

017 MAKING INFERENCES

An inference is a reasonable conclusion based on evidence.

Example:

Evidence: Your friend has a broken leg.
Inference: Your friend had an accident.

Writers often use details and examples to suggest what they mean rather than stating it directly. Readers must then infer meaning from the details.

Example:

Detail: Dr. Wang gave a lot of money to support programs for the arts, education, and medical care.
Inference: Dr. Wang was a very generous person.

018 PARAPHRASING

When you paraphrase, you put information and ideas into your own words. Paraphrasing is a good way to check your understanding of written material. It can also help you remember ideas and information.

Example:

(Text)
The boy had no father or mother.
(Paraphrase)
The boy was an orphan.

(Text)
In 1948, only three years after arriving in the United States, Wang earned a Ph.D. in Physics from Harvard University.
(Paraphrase)
Wang earned a doctoral degree after just three years in the United States.

019 PREDICTING

What is the weather going to be like tomorrow? What is the next paragraph in this reading going to be about? What is going to happen to the main character in this story? When you answer these questions, you are making predictions.

When you make a prediction, you use what you already know about a topic, person, or event. Using what you already know helps you to make a logical prediction.

Example:

The title of the article I am going to read is From Russia to America in 1980. *From the title, I predict that the article is about someone who came to America from Russia. Based on what I already know about Russia and America in 1980, I predict that the article might be about the problems this person had leaving Russia and coming to America.*

Making predictions helps you to focus on the material you are reading. You make a prediction and then you read to check if your prediction is correct.

020 PREVIEWING

The word *preview* means "to look before." To preview an article or story, look over the whole reading before you start to read.

- Look at the title and ask yourself questions about it. Then predict answers to your questions.

- Look at the pictures and predict what the article or story is about.

- Recall what you already know about the topic.

- Read the first paragraph and the last paragraph and try to figure out the main idea of the reading.

- Set a purpose for reading. Decide what you hope to find out as you read.

021 READING FOR SPECIFIC INFORMATION

Sometimes your purpose for reading is limited. You don't want to know everything; you only want a few pieces of information.

Example:

You have an article on the expansion of the Sahara Desert. Maybe you only want to know <u>how fast</u> the Sahara is expanding. Then, as you read, you look for numbers and periods of time, such as "two kilometers per year" or "one acre a month."

If you know what you are looking for, you can focus on the limited possibilities. You can read quickly by scanning for this information. (See 022 Scanning.)

022 SCANNING

Scanning means "to look quickly for specific information." Here is how you scan:

• Let your eyes move quickly down the page. Don't read every word.

• Slow down when you see words or phrases that might be important to you.

• Check (✓) or <u>underline</u> them, if you think they are important.

Scanning saves time if you are collecting specific information and ideas.

023 SUMMARIZING

When you summarize, you restate ideas and information briefly in your own words. A summary gives only the most important ideas and information.

Example:

(Text)
When An Wang came to the United States in 1945, he had already lost both of his parents and one sister. He had also lived through a civil war in China. But these troubles taught him an important lesson. By the time he left China, he believed that he could try to accomplish anything; nothing was impossible.

(Summary)
From his difficult and painful childhood, An Wang learned that he could try to do anything.

024 TAKING NOTES IN A CHART

Taking notes as you read helps you to organize and remember important information. When you take notes, write down the most important information only. Here is one type of chart you might use:

Main Ideas	Details
He had a difficult childhood.	His parents died. He lived through a civil war.
He accomplished a lot in his first 6 years in the U.S.	He got a Ph.D. He invented the magnetic core.

025 USING CONTEXT

Sometimes you can figure out the meaning of a difficult word by looking at the context—the other words in the sentence or surrounding sentences. Here are some context clues to look for:

A definition:

> It was at this time that he invented the **magnetic core.** <u>This device was a basic part of computer memory</u> until the use of microchips in the late 1960s.

> Before these discoveries, **famines**—<u>severe shortages of food</u>—caused many people to die from starvation.

A description:

> Her two sons were **peddlers.** <u>The oldest sold umbrellas and the youngest sold straw shoes.</u>

A comparison or contrast:

> He <u>loved</u> the first story, <u>but</u> he **despised** the second one.

A series:

> <u>Pizza,</u> **subs,** and <u>hamburgers</u> are popular in the United States.

> My grandfather was very **shy,** <u>never laughed loudly, and always spoke softly.</u>

> He often noticed the boy mopping the floors, <u>cheerfully</u> and **in good humor.**

Cause and effect:

> This house makes me **miserable** <u>because it is dark and gloomy.</u>

> They have trouble **getting along** <u>because they have different opinions about everything.</u>

Setting:

> After a late dinner, he put his rice on his A-frame and **set out for** his <u>brother's house</u>. It was a full moon and he could see the <u>path</u> clearly.

Example:

> At first he made **insulting** remarks, <u>such as "Hey! Wet Chicken! This is no place for a weakling!"</u>

> Blitzstein is warm and **gregarious.** <u>He likes to hear a good joke—and *loves* to tell a good story.</u>

Synonym:

> According to his lawyer, Abraham Lincoln was the most **reticent**—<u>secretive</u>—man that ever lived.

Critical Thinking Strategies

026 ANALYZING

You analyze in order to find out **why** something is the way it is. When you analyze something, you take it apart. You study each part and look for connections among the parts. When you analyze, you probably want to know the causes, effects, reasons, purposes, or consequences.

Example:

What was the cause of a particular automobile accident?
To analyze the cause, you might ask these questions:

- *Was more than one car involved in the accident?*
- *Was the road wet?*
- *What time of day did the accident happen?*
- *Was the driver alone? Was the driver tired? Was the driver drinking or on medication?*
- *What was the condition of the car before the accident?*

If you ask the right questions and get complete answers, you can make an analysis.

In your college courses, your teachers will expect you to analyze what you read. In order to analyze a text (the article, chapter, etc. that you are reading), here are some questions you might ask yourself:

- What/who is this text about?

- What is the context? What are the circumstances?

- What is the central issue or problem?

- What questions does the writer ask?

- What questions does the writer answer?

- What is the writer's central point(s)?

- So what? What does it all mean?

- How can you connect this text to other texts that you have read?

- What applications can you make to the world around you?

When you write, your readers need to be able to answer the same questions.

027 APPLYING WHAT YOU KNOW

Sometimes the best way to apply what you know is to "picture" the possibilities. You can build an image of results or consequences from what you know.

Example:

A young man you know is in love with a young woman, but she doesn't love him. (Sigh, sigh.)

What future possibilities can you picture?

1. *She changes her mind.*

2. *She doesn't change her mind, and he is unhappy for the rest of his life.*

3. *She doesn't change her mind, but he goes on with his life. Maybe he even finds someone new.*

How do you know the future possibilities? Well, you don't really know for sure; you have no crystal ball. Yet, you can imagine two or three possibilities from your own experience and/or other people's experience.

You also need to apply what you learn from your course work to the world around you. Maybe you know X and you apply what you know about X to Y. Maybe you never thought about a connection before.

Example:

You read this: Medical studies show that sick people get well faster if they feel cared for and loved.

You make the connection to your sick uncle. How can you apply what you've learned? Maybe you arrange to visit him more often and telephone him every day.

As you read and write, you need to make these connections and apply what you know.

028 CLASSIFYING

Classifying means "arranging and organizing into groups, classes, or categories."

Example:

At the supermarket, everything is arranged according to categories. This makes it possible for you to find what you want quickly.

apples
oranges } together as FRUIT
peaches

potatoes
carrots } together as VEGETABLES
onions

Writers often arrange their ideas in groups. In other words, they classify or categorize their thoughts and information.

Example:

You want to write about a friend. You might organize your ideas as follows:

brown eyes
beautiful smile
long, dark hair
tall and thin } together as PHYSICAL TRAITS

easy to please
likes people
curious
intelligent } together as PERSONALITY TRAITS

Readers can follow a writer's thinking if the ideas and information are classified logically.

029 COMPARING

Comparing is one way you can analyze a topic or situation: you look for similarities and differences. How are things, ideas, and people the **same?** How are they **different?** You need special language for comparing:

Maria is old**er than** Jose, her brother.

Few**er** people live in St. Louis **than** in Chicago.

I am **more** interested in history **than** in biology, but literature is my great**est** love.

Boston and New Orleans have a lot **in common: both** are old cities.

When you read, notice the writer's language. If you figure out that the writer is making a comparison, then you know to look for similarities and differences.

When you think about similarities and differences, it helps to visualize a Venn diagram. (See 009 Making a Venn Diagram.)

Example:

You are describing two of your friends in a letter to your parents, who have never met them. You might organize your thoughts this way:

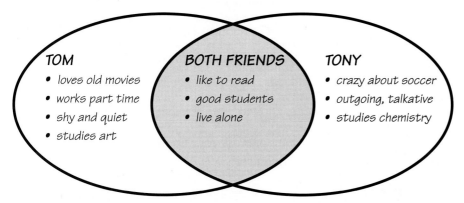

TOM
- *loves old movies*
- *works part time*
- *shy and quiet*
- *studies art*

BOTH FRIENDS
- *like to read*
- *good students*
- *live alone*

TONY
- *crazy about soccer*
- *outgoing, talkative*
- *studies chemistry*

Make a Venn diagram before you write a comparison. It will help you to organize your ideas.

030 EVALUATING

To answer questions such as these, you need to evaluate or make a judgement:

- What person in your life has influenced you **the most?**

- Which of your friends is your **best** friend?

- What is **the worst** movie you have ever seen?

- What did you **like or dislike** about this book?

- What is **the most** important quality in a mate?

Your evaluation is your opinion. There are no right or wrong answers to such questions. However, your reader expects you to <u>explain</u> your evaluation when you write.

Example:

You judge honesty to be the most important quality in a mate.

Your reasoning might begin like this:

> • *You need to build a relationship on trust.*
>
> • *For you to trust your mate, she/he has to be honest.*
>
> • *You must depend on your mate to tell the truth.*
>
> • *If your mate is honest, then you can trust her/him.*

It is important for you to express your opinions and then to explain them, to support them with reasons.

031 INTERPRETING

• What does something mean?

• What does it mean **to you?**

• **In your opinion,** what does it mean?

• What do **you** think?

• What is **your** reaction?

You interpret when you answer these questions: you talk about the **meaning or significance** of something.

An interpretation comes from inside your head. Two people may have two different interpretations of the same thing (a poem, word, book, movie, event, etc.) because they have different experiences in life, different values, and different knowledge.

Interpretations are neither right or wrong. Yet, you need to convince your reader that your interpretation is good by supporting it with facts, reasons, or evidence.

Example:

What does the Vietnam Memorial (in Washington D.C.) signify?

One interpretation: It signifies the tragedy of war, the waste of human life.

Possible reasons for this interpretation: (1) the 50,000(+) names of the dead engraved on the memorial show how many Americans died and (2) the open grief expressed by people when they visit the memorial

Your interpretation is important. State what you think and then support it by explaining why.

032 SYNTHESIZING

Synthesizing is the process of pulling pieces of information and ideas together. It might be in a new way. It might be for a new purpose.

When you pull together ideas from different sources, you might make something new as you add your own ideas and experiences.

Example:

You are interested in the family as a topic.

You read about the role of the <u>extended family</u> (different generations of the same family) in some cultures. You also read about the role of the <u>nuclear family</u> (mother, father, and children) in other cultures. You have your own experience to pull from; plus, you have interviewed several of your classmates.

You think about all you have learned and you see that there are different kinds of families. Maybe you look at what they have in common and you arrive at a new way of viewing the family. Maybe you argue in your writing that the structure of the family does not matter, as long as people living together love each other and take care of each other.

Synthesizing is a very important process for students in college. Your teachers will expect you to do a lot of reading and pull it all together in your own unique way.

CREDITS

Photography

p. xxvi	Morris/Perkins
p. xxvii	Sven Martson/Comstock
p. xxviii	Morris/Perkins
p. 2 top	Mike Mazzaschi/Stock Boston
p. 2 bottom	Judy Gelles/Stock Boston
p. 3	Rhoda Sidney/The Image Works
p. 6	Morris/Perkins
p. 7	Morris/Perkins—Courtesy of Boston College *Stylus*
p. 24 top	AP/Wide World Photos
p. 24 bottom	UPI/Bettmann
p. 27	Courtesy Wang Laboratories
p. 32	Morris/Perkins
p. 38	John Kaprielian/Photo Researchers
p. 39	John Kaprielian/Photo Researchers
p. 40	Jeffrey Dunn/Monkmeyer Press
p. 47 left	Cameron Davidson/Comstock
p. 47 middle	R. Michael Stuckey/Comstock
p. 47 right	Karen Rubin/FPG
p. 48	Frank Gordon/FPG
p. 49	David Bartuff/FPG
p. 51 left	Rob Crandall/Stock Boston
p. 51 right	John Maher/Stock Boston
p. 62	Stuart Cohen/Comstock
p. 63	Comstock
p. 70	Superstock
p. 72 top	Antman/The Image Works
p. 72 bottom left	Ulrike Welsh
p. 72 right	Ulrike Welsh
p. 88 left	Comstock
p. 88 right	Comstock
p. 90 bottom left	Hazel Hankin/Stock Boston
p. 90 top left	Superstock
p. 90 top right	Jack Spratt/The Image Works
p. 90 bottom right	Ulrike Welsch
p. 108 top	D. Greco/The Image Works
p. 108 bottom	George Malave/Stock Boston
p. 109	Steve & Mary Skjold Photographers
p. 120	Michael Lajoie Photography
p. 125	UPI/Bettmann
p. 130	Michael Weisbrot/Stock Boston
p. 131	Robert Kelley
p. 138	Alinari/Art Resource
p. 143 top left	Dick Luria/FPG
p. 143 bottom	Steven W. Jones/FPG
p. 143 top right	Maureen Fennelli/Comstock
p. 147	Danny Clinch
p. 153 left	The Bettmann Archive
p. 153 top right	Archive Photos/London Daily Express
p. 153 bottom right	Archive Photos/London Daily Express
p. 162	© 1994 Artist's Rights Society, NY/Vegap, Madrid

Illustration

Anne O'Brien: pp. 12–13, 74–75, 98–99, 112–13,
Stephanie Peterson: pp. 2–3, 4, 5, 18–19, 29, 42–43,
    92, 118–19, 160, 163
Len Shalansky: p. 54

Text